GUIDE TO GOOD PRACTICE

under the Hague Convention of 25 October 1980 on the Civil Aspects of International Child Abduction

PART I - CENTRAL AUTHORITY PRACTICE

GUIDE TO GOOD PRACTICE

under the Hague Convention of 25 October 1980 on the Civil Aspects of International Child Abduction

PART I - CENTRAL AUTHORITY PRACTICE

Published by
Family Law
A publishing imprint of Jordan Publishing Limited
21 St Thomas Street
Bristol BS1 6JS

For the Hague Conference on Private International Law
Permanent Bureau | Bureau Permanent
6, Scheveningseweg   2517 KT The Hague | La Haye   The Netherlands | Pays-Bas
telephone | téléphone +31 (0)70 363 3303   fax | télécopieur +31 (0)70 360 4867
e-mail | courriel secretariat@hcch.net   website | site internet http://www.hcch.net

British Library Cataloguing-in-Publication Data
A catalogue record for this book is available from the British Library.

ISBN 0 85308 8934

Printed in Great Britain by Hobbs The Printers Limited, Southampton

EXECUTIVE SUMMARY

TABLE OF CONTENTS

1. SUMMARY: KEY OPERATING PRINCIPLES

1.1 Resources and powers

Central Authorities should be given:

1.1.1 Sufficient powers
1.1.2 Qualified personnel
1.1.3 Adequate material resources, including modern means of communication to carry out their functions effectively

1.2 Co-operation

1.2.1 Co-operation between Central Authorities is essential to the effective working of the Convention
1.2.2 Improve co-operation through good communication which is timely, clear, and responsive to the matter raised
1.2.3 Improve co-operation through meetings and exchange of information about different legal and administrative systems
1.2.4 Improve co-operation by eliminating obstacles to the Convention

1.3 Communication

1.3.1 There is a fundamental need for clear and effective communication between Central Authorities
1.3.2 Central Authority contact details must be current
1.3.3 Provide prompt responses and use, as far as possible, modern rapid means of communication
1.3.4 Provide information about the practice and procedure in each country and, if feasible, establish a website
1.3.5 Keep each other informed about the operation of the Convention

1.4 Consistency

1.4.1 The use of the model form for applications is preferred
1.4.2 There should also be uniform standards for the type of information provided in applications, including:

- a statement of the legal and factual basis for the application, especially the habitual residence of the child, rights of custody and the exercise of those rights

- information on location of the child

1.4.3 Consistency in interpretation of key concepts in the Convention

1.5 Expeditious procedures

1.5.1 Speedy, prompt or expeditious action is required at all stages of the Hague Convention process
1.5.2 Failure to act promptly undermines the Convention
1.5.3 Interests of the child require expeditious action:

- to minimise disruption or dislocation to the child

- to minimise harm to the child

- to prevent or limit any advantage to the abductor by the passage of time

1.6   Transparency

- Throughout the Hague application process, there should be transparency in both legal process and administrative procedure

- Transparency in the administrative procedure requires that interested parties have access to information about those procedures

- Central Authorities should provide clear information about their country's processes and procedures

1.7   Progressive implementation

- All Central Authorities have had to review and revise their early procedures, as they gained more practical experience with the Convention, and obtained more information about practices in other countries

- This evolution in practices and procedures is recognised as progressive implementation. It requires that all Central Authorities, both established and developing, and their Contracting States, will take steps whenever possible to improve the operation of the Convention in their respective countries

2. SUMMARY: ESTABLISHING AND CONSOLIDATING THE CENTRAL AUTHORITY

2.1 Why?

2.1.1 The designation and establishment of a Central Authority is an obligation of the Convention under Article 6

2.1.2 Designation of "central" Central Authorities for Federal States is necessary

2.2 When?

2.2.1 The Central Authority should be designated at the time of ratification or accession to the Convention

2.2.2 The Central Authority must be established and ready to send and receive applications at the time the Convention enters into force for the Contracting State

2.3 Where?

2.3.1 The Central Authority is a position or office created to carry out the obligations and functions of the Convention

2.3.2 The Office of the Central Authority should have a connection with the subject matter of the Convention

2.3.3 The Office of the Central Authority should have strong links to the internal justice and welfare system

2.4 Who?

The personnel or staff of the Central Authority should be:

2.4.1 Sufficient in numbers to cope with the workload

2.4.2 Properly qualified and trained to understand the requirements of the Convention

2.4.3 Properly qualified and trained to understand how the Convention operates within their domestic legal and administrative framework

2.4.4 Of a suitable temperament to work co-operatively with foreign agencies and with children and parents in distress

2.4.5 Committed to achieving the goals of the Convention

2.4.6 Competent in relevant foreign language skills

2.4.7 Personnel who will remain for a reasonable period of time in their positions

2.5 What?

2.5.1 Equipment and materials for all Central Authorities.

The minimum level of essential equipment and materials includes:

- telephone

- fax machine

- stationery

- computer/word processor or typewriter

- copy of the Convention

- translation of the Convention into the national language

- copy of applicable implementing legislation or procedures

- copy of the Explanatory Report to the Convention by Elisa Pérez-Vera

- list of lawyers or administrative officials who are able to represent the applicant in any Convention proceedings

- written procedures for handling Convention applications

- list of qualified translators to translate applications

- the Guide to Good Practice

- full contact details for all other Central Authorities

- a register for maintenance of statistics

2.5.2   Equipment and materials in well-resourced Central Authorities

A well resourced Central Authority will have, in addition to the items listed above:

- email facilities

- internet access

- library/collection of Convention literature

- materials for education programmes

- office procedures manual for Convention applications

- arrangements through Interpol, local police or Central Authority personnel on call, to provide 24 hour contact

- strategic plan for twinning arrangements

- electronic case management system

3. SUMMARY: ABDUCTION APPLICATIONS (OUTGOING): ROLE OF THE REQUESTING CENTRAL AUTHORITY

OUTLINE OF PROCEDURES

Preparing and sending applications

3.1 Obtain information about procedures in the requested country

3.2 Check that the application is complete and in an acceptable form for the requested country

3.3 Check that the application satisfies Convention requirements

3.4 Discuss the operation of the Convention with the applicant

3.5 Provide information about relevant laws

3.6 Ensure all essential supporting documents are included

3.7 Provide a translation of the application and all essential documents

3.8 Ensure the application is sent to the correct postal address or fax number or email address of the requested Central Authority

3.9 Send the original application by priority mail, and fax or email an advance copy of the application

3.10 If the application is very urgent, explain the reasons for the urgency

Assisting and responding to the requested Central Authority

3.11 If the requested Central Authority requires additional information, ensure that all the information is provided promptly

3.12 Advise the requested Central Authority if there are difficulties in meeting their deadlines

3.13 Be reasonable about requests for follow-up information

3.14 Monitor progress of the application

3.15 Assist the applicant to obtain an Article 15 declaration or determination if necessary

Procedures following return order

3.16 Additional enforcement action is sometimes needed in particular countries

3.17 Be aware of the appeals process in the requested country

3.18 Co-operate with the requested Central Authority to facilitate a safe return of the child, and where necessary, the accompanying parent

3.19 Provide requested Central Authority with confirmation of the return of the child

3.20 Verify agreed arrangements with the appropriate protection and welfare authorities in the requesting country are in place when the child returns

3.21 If conditions were imposed or undertakings given with the return order, take whatever steps are appropriate within the limits of the Central Authority's powers, to ensure that the conditions are met or the undertakings are fulfilled

4. SUMMARY: ABDUCTION APPLICATIONS (INCOMING): ROLE OF THE REQUESTED CENTRAL AUTHORITY

OUTLINE OF PROCEDURES

Receiving and acknowledging applications

4.1	Observe internal or external timeframes
4.2	Applications may be received by mail or by fax or email
4.3	Register the receipt of the application on an internal register
4.4	Acknowledge receipt of the application
4.5	Check the application to ensure Convention requirements are satisfied
4.6	If additional information or documents are required, advise the requesting Central Authority in the acknowledgement letter/email or in a follow-up letter/email
4.7	If the application is very urgent, or if the 12 month deadline for a mandatory return is imminent, make every effort to expedite matters more quickly than usual
4.8	Inform the court of the Article 16 limitations on custody hearings
4.9	If the application will not be accepted, inform the requesting Central Authority of reasons

Actions following acceptance of applications

4.10	Locate the child and confirm that he/she is actually in the requested country
4.11	If the child is not located, return the application; if the child has moved to another territory, forward the application as appropriate
4.12	If the application meets the Convention requirements, consider if a voluntary return is appropriate and feasible
4.13	Arrange legal representation for the applicant or assist the applicant to obtain legal representation
4.14	Provide the requesting Central Authority with follow-up information about action taken on behalf of the applicant
4.15	Take steps to prevent further harm to the child or prejudice to interested parties
4.16	Initiate or facilitate legal proceedings. Legal proceedings may be commenced even if a voluntary return is contemplated
4.17	Applicants should not be required to attend court hearings in the requested country, unless it is absolutely essential and the court requires it
4.18	Monitor progress of the application
4.19	Inform requesting Central Authority as soon as a court decision is known
4.20	Ensure that the requesting Central Authority or the applicant is aware of his/her rights of appeal

Practical arrangements for the return of the child

4.21 Consider the practical arrangements for return of the child. These arrangements should be under consideration well before a return order is made

4.22 If conditions or undertakings are to be included in the return order, the Central Authority should be consulted by the applicant's lawyer about the reasonableness of the conditions or undertakings

4.23 If a return is to be ordered, the Central Authority may be consulted on any issues or concerns about the safe return of the child or parent

4.24 Ensure that the abductor who wishes to return with the child is provided with information about services or assistance available in the requesting country

4.25 Assistance with enforcement of a return order may be sought from police or other agencies

4.26 Get confirmation from the requesting country that the child (and parent) has (have) returned

4.27 Maximise opportunities to inform the professions about the principles and procedures of the Hague Convention

5.   SUMMARY: ACCESS APPLICATIONS: ROLE OF REQUESTING AND REQUESTED CENTRAL AUTHORITIES

Preliminary observations

- Article 21 facilitates access arrangements and requires Central Authorities to remove, as far as possible, all obstacles to the exercise of such rights

- Article 7(f) imposes an obligation to take all appropriate measures to make arrangements in a proper case for organising or securing the effective exercise of rights of access

- Articles 7 and 21 together require Central Authorities to co-operate in promoting the peaceful enjoyment of access rights

- specific measures that Central Authorities can take depend on the nature and extent of their powers to act

- deficiencies in the Convention in securing protection for rights of access have been recognised

A.   OUTLINE OF PROCEDURE FOR THE REQUESTING CENTRAL AUTHORITY (OUTGOING APPLICATIONS)

Preparing and sending applications

5.1   Obtain information about procedures in the requested country
5.2   Check that the application is complete and in an acceptable form for the requested country
5.3   Check that the application satisfies Convention requirements
5.4   Provide information about relevant laws
5.5   Ensure all essential supporting documents are included
5.6   Provide a translation of the application and all essential documents
5.7   Ensure the application is sent to the correct mailing address, fax number or email address of the requested Central Authority
5.8   Send the original application by priority mail, and fax or email an advance copy of the application
5.9   If the application is very urgent, highlight the reasons for the urgency

Assisting and responding to the requested Central Authority

5.10   If the requested Central Authority requires additional information, ensure that all the information is provided promptly
5.11   Advise the requested Central Authority if there are difficulties in meeting their deadlines
5.12   Be reasonable about requests for follow-up information
5.13   Monitor progress of the application

Assisting with the effective exercise of access rights

5.14 Assistance available in the requesting country

5.15 Assistance if access is to take place in the requesting country

5.16 Co-operate with the requested Central Authority to ensure agreed arrangements are observed

B. OUTLINE OF PROCEDURE FOR THE REQUESTED CENTRAL AUTHORITY (INCOMING APPLICATIONS)

Receiving and acknowledging applications

5.17 Establishing timeframes for dealing with applications

5.18 Applications may be received by mail, fax or email

5.19 Register the receipt of the application on an internal register

5.20 Acknowledge receipt of the application

5.21 Check the application to ensure Convention requirements are satisfied

5.22 If additional information or documents are required, advise the requesting Central Authority in the acknowledgement letter/email or in a follow-up letter/email

5.23 If the Central Authority decides not to accept the application, inform the requesting Central Authority of the reasons

Actions following acceptance of the application

5.24 Locate the child and confirm that he/she is actually in the requested country

5.25 If the child is not located, return the application

5.26 If the application meets the Convention requirements, consider if voluntary contact arrangements are appropriate and feasible

5.27 Arrange legal representation for the applicant or assist the applicant to obtain legal representation

Assisting with the effective exercise of access rights

5.28 Provide the requesting Central Authority with follow-up information about action taken on behalf of the applicant

5.29 Ensure that the procedures permitted by the administrative and judicial system of the requested country are followed

5.30 Take steps to prevent further harm to the child or prejudice to interested parties, if feasible and appropriate

5.31 Attendance of applicants at court hearings in the requested country will depend on the individual circumstances of the case

5.32 Monitor progress of the application

5.33 Assist with implementing or enforcing access orders

6.   **SUMMARY: OTHER IMPORTANT FUNCTIONS AND ISSUES FOR CENTRAL AUTHORITIES**

6.1   **The maintenance of statistics**

- Central Authorities should maintain accurate Convention statistics

- Central Authorities should make annual returns of statistics to the Permanent Bureau

- A statistical database (INCASTAT) will be established as a complement to the International Child Abduction Database (INCADAT)

- Collecting and sending reliable statistics is an additional demand on the resources of Central Authorities. If necessary they should seek assistance to develop accurate statistical recording processes

6.2   **Education and training**

- The Convention generally works well in the interests of children and meets the needs for which it was drafted

- However, education of the general public and the legal and welfare professions about the Convention remains a priority, and Central Authorities should take an active role to achieve this goal

- Preventing child abduction through public education is important and Central Authorities should try to reach the widest audience through various methods of information dissemination

6.3   **Issues surrounding the safe return of children and parents**

- Concerning safe return orders, the issue is to obtain in the requesting jurisdiction any provisional protective measures prior to the return of the child

- Concerning criminal proceedings, the issue is to take into account the impact of a criminal prosecution for child abduction on the possibility of achieving a return of the child

- Concerning immigration matters, the issue is to take measures to ensure that generally the abducting parent will be permitted to re-enter the requesting Country to participate in custody or access proceedings

- Concerning the provision of legal aid and advice, the issue is to take measures to ensure that parents have access to a country's legal system to adequately present their case in custody proceedings following a child's return

6.4   Repatriation

- Central Authorities should give consideration to practical forms of assistance for repatriating children to their habitual residence country

6.5   Twinning arrangements

- A "twinning" arrangement could arise if a developing Central Authority seeks assistance from an experienced Central Authority to provide advice, materials, training and possibly an exchange of personnel for practical training and experience

6.6   The 1996 Hague Convention on Child Protection

- The 1996 Convention has potential advantages as an adjunct to the 1980 Convention, and Contracting States are recommended to consider ratification or accession.

6.7   Prevention

6.7.1 Information

6.7.2 Education

6.7.3 Co-operation

6.7.4 Legislation

6.8   Enforcement

The enforcement of return orders will be improved if the following matters are addressed in each Contracting State:

- Effective mechanisms for enforcement are included in implementing measures, including implementing legislation

- Co-operation between the judicial authority and the enforcement agency

- Clear directions in the return order about how the return arrangements are to be effected

- Any necessary precautionary measures to reduce the risk of flight by the abductor with the child after the return order is made

CENTRAL AUTHORITY PRACTICE

TABLE OF CONTENTS

The Guide

5. ACCESS APPLICATIONS: ROLE OF REQUESTING AND REQUESTED CENTRAL AUTHORITIES

Preliminary observations

A.   ROLE OF REQUESTING CENTRAL AUTHORITY

B.   ROLE OF REQUESTED CENTRAL AUTHORITY

INTRODUCTION

There are now more than seventy States Parties to the *Hague Convention of 25 October 1980 on the Civil Aspects of International Child Abduction.* The States Parties meet together periodically in a Special Commission organised by the Permanent Bureau of the Hague Conference on Private International Law, to review, and make recommendations on, practice under the Convention. The reports of these Special Commission meetings, which have been held in 1989, 1993, 1997 and 2001, are available on the website of the Hague Conference on Private International Law at <http://www.hcch.net/e/conventions/reports28e.html>.

During the fourth of these review meetings, held at The Hague on 22-28 March 2001, the following recommendation was made:

> *"Contracting States to the Convention should co-operate with each other and with the Permanent Bureau to develop a good practice guide which expands on Article 7 of the Convention. This guide would be a practical, "how-to" guide, to help implement the Convention. It would concentrate on operational issues and be targeted particularly at new Contracting States. It would not be binding nor infringe upon the independence of the judiciary. The methodology should be left to the Permanent Bureau."*

The project to establish a Guide to Good Practice under the 1980 Convention began with the completion in 2002 of Part I - Central Authority Practice and Part II - Implementing Measures. A recommendation was made at the Special Commission concerning the *Hague Convention of 25 October 1980 on the Civil Aspects of International Child Abduction* held at The Hague from 27 September to 1 October 2002 to develop a Guide for transfrontier access/contact matters. The Permanent Bureau was also requested to prepare reports on the need for Guides covering prevention of abductions, enforcement of return orders, and judicial co-operation.

● ● ● ●

Part I of the Guide to Good Practice is primarily directed towards Central Authorities, but for some topics, it has relevance to their Contracting States. It is one objective of this Guide to collate a range of good Convention practices, developed through experience and by trial and error over the years. The Guide is designed to assist both new and established Central Authorities and to save them time and effort by putting at their disposal a range of tried and tested practices which have resulted in effective implementation of the Convention in countries in which they have been adopted.

Some Central Authorities may find the Guide is a useful tool in discussions with their own authorities about the need for additional resources or changes to legislation. The Guide should also help to resolve differences and unify practice among Central Authorities.

This Guide attempts to take into account the experience and resources and case load of both new and established Central Authorities. It is acknowledged that Central Authorities may be given varying roles within their respective Contracting States, and that their powers and functions will often differ in detail under the national laws or provisions which establish them. Nevertheless, the Convention does place certain core obligations on Central Authorities or their intermediaries (*see*, in particular, Article 7), and it is the responsibility of the Central Authority to have procedures in place to ensure that those obligations are carried out, even when it is not the Central Authority itself which undertakes the specific function or obligation.

The Guide attempts to set realistic standards for new and developing Central Authorities to achieve, bearing in mind that they may have limited resources at the outset, and even for an indefinite period. Even among more established Central Authorities, implementation of the Guide will also vary depending on the legal capacities of individual Central Authorities.

Nothing in this Guide may be construed as binding on particular Central Authorities; however, all Central Authorities are encouraged to review their own practices, and where appropriate and feasible, to change them. For both established and developing Central Authorities, the implementation of the Convention should be seen as a continuing, progressive or incremental process of improvement.

● ● ● ●

The development of this Part of the Guide was assisted by close consultations with Central Authorities. The Permanent Bureau would like to thank the many Central Authorities whose accumulated wisdom and experience has contributed to the Guide. Particular thanks are due to Jennifer Degeling, Principal Legal Officer and head of the Australian Federal Central Authority who, while on secondment during 2002 to the Permanent Bureau (thanks to the generosity of the Government of Australia), has carried out the principal work on this Part of the Guide. The Permanent Bureau would also like to extend its gratitude to those States whose contributions to the supplementary budget of the Hague Conference have made possible the development and publication of this Part of the Guide.

● ● ● ●

Part I of the Guide to Good Practice was prepared by the Permanent Bureau and then considered and approved by a Special Commission concerning the *Hague Convention of 25 October 1980 on the Civil Aspects of International Child Abduction* held at The Hague from 27 September to 1 October 2002.

GLOSSARY

Conditions: The requested courts sometimes place conditions on an order for the return of a child to a Convention country. Conditions are, in effect, pre-conditions to be met usually by the left behind parent, before the child will be returned. If the conditions are incorporated into the terms of the return order, they are enforceable as a court order.

Court settlement: In civil law systems, a court settlement is the equivalent of a common law consent order. The parties agree to the terms of a settlement of the issue, and the court approves the settlement and gives it the force of an order of the court.

Implementing legislation: Implementing legislation refers to the range of instruments having the force of law. It is intended to cover a variety of instruments found in civil law and common law systems, such as acts of parliament, statutes, civil or criminal codes, all delegated legislation such as rules and regulations, rules of court.

Implementing measures: Implementing measures refer to the range of legislative, judicial and administrative measures or procedures necessary to establish the essential legal and administrative framework to fully implement the Convention.

Mirror orders: These are identical or similar orders made by the courts in both the requested and requesting countries. As such, they are fully enforceable and effective in both countries.

Rules of Court: These are a feature of common law systems. A committee of judges and administrators draft procedural rules for the court. The rules provide detailed instructions to deal with various matters such as the manner and time for filing of documents. The Rules of Court are tabled in the legislature, and have the force of law.

Undertakings: An undertaking is a promise, or commitment, or assurance given by a person to a court to do, or not do, certain things. Requested courts in certain jurisdictions will accept, or even require, undertakings from the left behind parent to overcome obstacles to the return of a child. An undertaking formally given to a court will be enforceable in the jurisdiction where it is given, but not usually elsewhere.

1.   SUMMARY: KEY OPERATING PRINCIPLES

1.1   Resources and powers

Central Authorities should be given:

1.1.1   Sufficient powers

1.1.2   Qualified personnel

1.1.3   Adequate material resources, including modern means of communication to carry out their functions effectively

1.2   Co-operation

1.2.1   Co-operation between Central Authorities is essential to the effective working of the Convention

1.2.2   Improve co-operation through good communication which is timely, clear, and responsive to the matter raised

1.2.3   Improve co-operation through meetings and exchange of information about different legal and administrative systems

1.2.4   Improve co-operation by eliminating obstacles to the Convention

1.3   Communication

1.3.1   There is a fundamental need for clear and effective communication between Central Authorities

1.3.2   Central Authority contact details must be current

1.3.3   Provide prompt responses and use, as far as possible, modern rapid means of communication

1.3.4   Provide information about the practice and procedure in each country and, if feasible, establish a website

1.3.5   Keep each other informed about the operation of the Convention

1.4   Consistency

1.4.1   The use of the model form for applications is preferred

1.4.2   There should also be uniform standards for the type of information provided in applications, including:

- a statement of the legal and factual basis for the application, especially the habitual residence of the child, rights of custody and the exercise of those rights

- information on location of the child

1.4.3   Consistency in interpretation of key concepts in the Convention

1.5   Expeditious procedures

1.5.1   Speedy, prompt or expeditious action is required at all stages of the Hague Convention process

1.5.2   Failure to act promptly undermines the Convention

1.5.3   Interests of the child require expeditious action:

- to minimise disruption or dislocation to the child

- to minimise harm to the child

- to prevent or limit any advantage to the abductor by the passage of time

1.6   Transparency

- Throughout the Hague application process, there should be transparency in both legal process and administrative procedure

- Transparency in the administrative procedure requires that interested parties have access to information about those procedures

- Central Authorities should provide clear information about their country's processes and procedures

1.7   Progressive implementation

- All Central Authorities have had to review and revise their early procedures, as they gained more practical experience with the Convention, and obtained more information about practices in other countries

- This evolution in practices and procedures is recognised as progressive implementation. It requires that all Central Authorities, both established and developing, and their Contracting States, will take steps whenever possible to improve the operation of the Convention in their respective countries

1. KEY OPERATING PRINCIPLES

The Central Authorities designated by the Contracting States play a vital role in making the Convention function effectively.

A number of key operating principles should guide every Contracting State and every Central Authority in applying the Convention. These may be summarised under the following headings:

- resources and powers

- co-operation

- communication

- consistency

- expeditious procedures

- transparency

- progressive implementation

The key operating principles are interdependent. Each relies on one or more of the other key operating principles to be fully effective. For example, without adequate resources, it will be difficult to comply with any of the other key operating principles. Similarly, expeditious procedures depend on adequate human and material resources as well as on good communication and co-operation.

1.1 Resources and powers

Central Authorities should be given a mandate which is sufficiently broad, and the qualified personnel and the resources, including modern means of communication, necessary to act dynamically and carry out their functions effectively. Central Authorities should have a regular staff, able to develop expertise in the operation of the Convention.[1]

The maintenance of a regular staff may be problematic in Central Authorities with a very small number of cases. The difficulties in developing a workable system in such circumstances are recognised. One way to minimise the problem, especially if there is no continuity of personnel, is to ensure that the office develops a procedure manual for the Convention, which can be followed by anyone who is required to fulfil the Central Authority's obligations. The Guide to Good Practice should form part of the procedure manual.

1.1.1 Sufficient powers

The obligations imposed on Central Authorities by the Convention can be quite onerous. These obligations are summarised in Appendix 2. The implementing

---

[1] Conclusion 1.1, Fourth Special Commission.

legislation or administrative arrangements of a Contracting State must make provision for the Central Authority to carry out its international obligations effectively. The Central Authority should have sufficient powers to do more than simply send or receive applications. The implementing legislation of a number of countries has given their Central Authorities wide powers to carry out their Convention obligations.[2] The implementing legislation of these countries may be amended from time to time to expand the powers of the Central Authority where new developments or Convention practice make it necessary or desirable to do so.

1.1.2 Qualified personnel

The desirable qualities and qualifications of Central Authority personnel are described in some detail in Chapter 2 under the heading "Who?". Proper training and an appropriate temperament for this work are essential.

The importance of having continuity with personnel must also be emphasised. Over a period of time, long term personnel are able to develop an invaluable body of knowledge and expertise in the requirements, not only of the operation of the Convention in their own country, but of the legal and administrative systems of many other countries. They also build up good relations with other Central Authorities which enhance co-operation and communication.

It is a fact of life that in the civil service, where most Central Authorities are located, staff rotations and promotions are commonplace. A succession plan should be developed in Central Authorities, whereby training of new personnel may start before the departure of experienced personnel. Where this is not possible, a training manual and a Convention procedures manual for the office should be prepared, to "capture" the knowledge and experience of departing personnel.

1.1.3 Adequate material resources

Together with sufficient powers and sufficient numbers of qualified personnel in the Central Authority there must be adequate material resources to permit the personnel to carry out their essential functions. The essential and desirable resources for Central Authorities are described in detail in Chapter 2.5 under the heading "What?".

Naturally, the resources required will depend on the number and complexity of applications, as well as on the level of involvement of the Central Authority with individual applications. Resources for the Central Authority should include modern, rapid means of communication.[3]

1.2 Co-operation

1.2.1 Good co-operation is essential for the Convention's operation

Co-operation between Central Authorities is essential to the effective working of the Convention. Lack of co-operation between Central Authorities leads to a lack of

---

[2] *See* Guide to Good Practice, Part II - Implementing Measures, Chapter 3.
[3] Conclusion 1.4, Fourth Special Commission.

confidence, misunderstandings and mistrust between the Central Authority personnel, with subsequent difficulties in the implementation of the Convention in each Contracting State.

The importance of co-operation is highlighted by the specific inclusion in Article 7 of an obligation to co-operate. Good co-operation can be achieved by observing the good practices in dealing with applications described in Chapters 3 to 5.

When Central Authorities develop office procedures for dealing with applications, they should consider how their procedures can improve co-operation. Article 7 also requires Central Authorities to promote co-operation between the Central Authority and local agencies such as police, social workers and courts, or agencies such as Interpol. Without the assistance of this essential network of relevant agencies, the objects of the Convention will be defeated. The Central Authority should take responsibility for developing this network, and for keeping individuals and agencies informed of Convention issues. Chapter 6.2 contains suggestions for education and training of network personnel in Convention issues.

1.2.2 *Improving co-operation through good communication*

Co-operation is enhanced by good communication: communication which is timely, clear, and responsive to the matter raised. In this context, the ability to communicate with Central Authority personnel in their own language should not be underestimated as an aid to good co-operation.

1.2.3 *Improving co-operation through meetings and exchange of information*

Co-operation is also enhanced when Central Authority personnel are able to meet and discuss matters of mutual interest and concern. Such personal contact, through conferences, Special Commissions, and bilateral or regional meetings, contributes enormously to an understanding of and respect for different legal and administrative systems. Meetings are most effective when there is active participation in meetings by persons who are knowledgeable about the law and administrative procedures of the Convention, as well as the legal and policy framework of their country for the Convention's implementation.

1.2.4 *Improving co-operation by eliminating obstacles to the application of the Convention*

Central Authorities are required by Article 7(i) to take all appropriate measures, as far as possible, to eliminate any obstacles to the application of the Convention. Within their respective countries, Central Authorities should take an active role in informing the appropriate Government agency of obstacles and difficulties they have experienced or anticipate in the future in applying the Convention.

Regarding obstacles as between Contracting States, a number of solutions are available:

- direct discussions may be held by the Central Authorities of the two affected countries (and if necessary, by diplomatic channel);

- issues may be raised for discussion at Special Commission meetings;

- systemic problems could be discussed at regional meetings of Central Authorities;

- a neutral body, such as the Permanent Bureau, may be invited to assist in a resolution of a particular problem or problems;

- an independent expert from a third country could be asked to give an opinion on the matter.

See also Chapter 4.9 on "Reasons for refusing to accept an application".

1.3 Communication

Confidentiality of communications is important. The applicant should be aware that confidentiality of personal information cannot always be guaranteed in the requested country's administrative and legal procedures, particularly when email communications are being used.

1.3.1 Clear and effective communication

The fundamental need for clear and effective communication and co-operation between Central Authorities, especially in individual cases, must be emphasised.[4]

1.3.2 Central Authority contact details

To facilitate effective and efficient communication between Central Authorities, the Permanent Bureau of the Hague Conference on Private International Law compiles a list of Central Authority contact persons, their contact details and any foreign languages spoken. This information is on the Hague Conference website,[5] it is regularly updated and will be sent by mail to any Central Authority without Internet access.

Contracting States should inform the Permanent Bureau promptly of the contact details of their Central Authority(ies), and Central Authorities should inform the Permanent Bureau promptly of the names of contact persons, of the means by which they may be contacted and of their languages of communication. Central Authorities should promptly inform the Permanent Bureau of any changes in these details.[6] Central Authorities should also inform the Permanent Bureau of any difficulties experienced in establishing contact with other Central Authorities. These are important aspects of "keeping each other informed" as required in Article 7(i).

Some Central Authorities also send a letter, fax or email to all other Central Authorities to notify them of significant changes, such as a new address, new telephone or fax numbers, or email addresses.

---

[4] *See* Conclusions 1.3-1.8, Fourth Special Commission.
[5] <http://www.hcch.net>.
[6] Conclusion 1.2, Fourth Special Commission.

1.3.3 Prompt responses and rapid communication

Central Authorities should acknowledge receipt of an application immediately and endeavour to provide follow-up information rapidly. Central Authorities should reply promptly to communications from other Central Authorities.[7] These issues are discussed in more detail in Chapters 3 to 5, which cover the handling of incoming and outgoing abduction and access applications.

Central Authorities should, as far as possible, use modern rapid means of communication in order to expedite proceedings, bearing in mind the requirements of confidentiality.[8]

Conclusion 1.4 recognises the advantages and disadvantages of technology such as email. Its prime advantages are ease and speed. Its disadvantages are lack of security, and a possible loss of speed when the addressee is unexpectedly absent from the office.

Central Authority personnel who correspond directly by email should be aware of a potential problem, especially if urgent requests for additional information or documents are sent by email. An email message sent to a particular person will not always be seen by any other officer in the Central Authority. If the message is urgent, requiring an immediate response, and the email recipient is absent for the day, no other officer may see the email to take appropriate action. Therefore it is advisable when sending extremely urgent emails, to consider sending the email to a second Central Authority officer as well, or sending a fax.

Some Central Authorities avoid this problem by having a central child abduction email address.[9] Then, emails may go to both the personal addressee and the central email address. In other Central Authorities, all the emails go through a central point for scanning, whether addressed to a particular person or not.

1.3.4 Provide information about the practice and procedure in each country and, if feasible, establish and regularly update a website

It is clear that greater access to, or exchange of, information about the practice and procedure in each country on all aspects of the operation of the Convention will minimise the demands on the Central Authority personnel, and will improve understanding and co-operation between countries. This is particularly true in relation to information about the administrative and legal processes for return and access applications in each country. If a Contracting State has specific requirements for particular documents or information to accompany an application, these must be made known to other Central Authorities.

Where information is intended for dissemination to other Central Authorities or foreign citizens, it would be desirable to present this information in either or both of the official languages of the Hague Conference, that is, French and English.

---

[7] Conclusion 1.3, Fourth Special Commission.
[8] Conclusion 1.4, Fourth Special Commission.
[9] The German Central Authority has a central email address.

Each Central Authority is encouraged, where this is feasible, to establish and regularly update a website, details of which should be furnished to the Permanent Bureau for the purpose of establishing a link with the Hague Conference website.[10]

It is recommended that each Central Authority should publish, on its website if possible and/or by other means, such as a brochure or flyer (the precise format being a matter for the Central Authority), information concerning at least the following matters:

- the other Contracting States in relation to whom the Convention is in effect;

- the means by which a missing child may be located;

- the designation and contact details for the Central Authority;

- application procedures (for return and access), documentary requirements, any standard forms employed and any language requirements;

- details, where applicable, of how to apply for legal aid or otherwise for the provision of legal service;

- the judicial procedures, including appeals procedures, which apply to return applications;

- enforcement options and procedures for return and access orders;

- any special requirements which may arise in the course of the proceedings (*e.g.* with regard to matters of evidence);

- information concerning the services applicable for the protection of a returning child (and accompanying parent, where relevant), and concerning applications for legal aid for, or the provision of legal services to, the accompanying parent on return; information, if applicable, concerning liaison judges.[11]

It is also recognised that a website is not feasible for every country, and other means of exchanging and publishing information about a range of Convention matters are encouraged. For example, a booklet, pamphlet, brochure or flyer could be printed and distributed. Any published material should be sent to the Permanent Bureau so that reference can be made to it on the Hague Conference website. Whatever the methods available to disseminate information, each Central Authority should provide information on laws and procedures in their respective States, including details of child protection/welfare agencies and, where applicable, how "mirror orders" can be made and enforced.

Although resources will be required to develop a website or brochure, there will be considerable long term savings in time and resources if important information is freely available and easily accessible.

---

[10] Conclusion 1.7, Fourth Special Commission.
[11] Conclusion 1.8, Fourth Special Commission.

1.3.5 *Keep each other informed about the operation of this Convention*

Article 7(i) contains the requirement for Central Authorities to "keep each other informed with respect to the operation of this Convention." This implies that any new developments affecting the operation of the Convention should be reported to other Contracting States.

An important aspect of this obligation is to maintain reliable statistics of Convention cases, and send them annually to the Permanent Bureau. This task will become even more important when the Statistical Database of Convention Cases (INCASTAT) is established, to complement the International Child Abduction Database of Convention decisions (INCADAT). *See also* Chapter 6.1 "Maintenance of Statistics".

Equally important is the responsibility of each Contracting State to actively participate in the regular reviews of the operation of the 1980 Convention during Special Commission meetings.

Central Authorities may be requested to complete detailed Questionnaires for these Special Commission meetings or for other projects being conducted by the Permanent Bureau. Central Authorities are urged to co-operate fully in these exercises, so that any analysis of the operation of the Convention will be based on the most comprehensive and current data possible.

1.4 Consistency

1.4.1 *The use of the model form for a request for return is preferred*

The model form for a request for return is preferred and its use is encouraged. A copy of the form is at Appendix 3.1. An electronic copy of the form can be found on the Hague website at <http://www.hcch.net/e/conventions/menu28e.html> in the document entitled "Recommendations".[12] A copy of a form for a request for access, based on the model return form, is at Appendix 3.2.

Central Authorities are strongly urged to use the model form because:

- processing of applications may be quicker;

- checking the application for compliance with the Convention is easier;

- essential information will not be omitted;

- it is universally accepted and understood;

- it avoids confusion for the requested authorities.

Occasionally, the form may have to be modified to satisfy particular requirements of the law and procedure of the requested country. Where two countries have a high volume of cases between them, they should co-operate to modify the forms sent to each other

---

[12] *See also* Model form for the Request for Return recommended by the Fourteenth Session of the Hague Conference (Actes et documents, (*Proceedings*) XIV ème Session, p. 423).

to take account of any specific requirements of their national law or procedure. This will increase speed and efficiency in handling applications.

1.4.2 Uniformity of information provided in applications

There is an absolute minimum standard of information needed to allow a requested Central Authority to be satisfied that an application comes within the Convention. This is evident from the model application form which sets out the basic requirements.

The requesting Central Authority should ensure that each application is accompanied by a sufficient statement of the legal and factual basis on which the application rests, in particular concerning the matters of the habitual residence of the child, rights of custody and the exercise of those rights, as well as detailed information on location of the child.[13]

1.4.3 Consistency in interpretation of terms

The key concepts which determine the scope of the Convention are not dependent for their meaning on any single legal system. Thus the expression "rights of custody", for example, does not coincide with any particular concept of custody in a domestic law, but draws its meaning from the definitions, structure and purposes of the Convention.[14] *See also* Guide to Good Practice, Part II - Implementing Measures, Chapters 1 and 8.

Central Authorities are encouraged to adopt any generally accepted usage and interpretation of Convention terms when carrying out their functions. *See also* Chapter 4.9 on "Reasons for refusing to accept an application". The International Child Abduction Database (INCADAT) is intended to facilitate consistency in interpretation of the Convention. Central Authorities should take all possible steps to inform the legal profession in their respective countries about the purpose and availability of INCADAT.[15]

1.5 Expeditious procedures

1.5.1 Expeditious procedures are essential at all stages of the Convention process

Speed is of the essence in Hague abduction matters. Expeditious procedure is a key operating principle for any person or body involved in the implementation of the Convention. This is clear from the objects of the Convention as set out in Article 1, to secure the prompt return of children. It is also clear from the general direction in Article 2 to use the most expeditious procedures possible, and in Article 11 to act expeditiously in proceedings for the return of children.

To encourage expeditious procedures, Article 23 of the Convention removes any requirement for legalisation of documents or similar formalities.

---

[13] Conclusion 1.6, Fourth Special Commission.
[14] Conclusion 2, Second Special Commission.
[15] INCADAT may be accessed at <http://www.incadat.com>. It is possible to apply for a free username and password on the "Welcome" page through the link entitled "password".

1.5.2 *Failure to act promptly undermines the Convention*

The most contentious issue surrounding implementation of the Convention concerns delay, in processing applications, resolving matters in court, or enforcing return orders. The need for speed at all stages of the process cannot be over-emphasised.

The four meetings of the Special Commission to date have all reiterated and endorsed conclusions and recommendations to the effect that Central Authorities must have adequate powers and resources to expeditiously handle requests for return of children or for access.[16]

Many Contracting States have expressed concerns about delays and excessively complex procedures used by Central Authorities in processing cases, in responding to communications, and in referring cases to court. An essential step that minimises these obstacles, and achieves speedy or prompt action, is to develop clear and effective administrative and legal procedures for handling Convention applications. This should be done at an early stage of implementation.

1.5.3 *Interests of the child require expeditious action*

The Preamble to the Convention states that the interests of children are paramount, and that the Convention's purpose is to protect them from the harmful effects of abduction. Experience has shown that speedy, prompt or expeditious action under the Hague Convention is a critical factor in protecting children's interests.

An expedited process will:

▪ minimise disruption or dislocation to the child taken from its familiar environment;

▪ minimise harm to the child caused by separation from the other parent;

▪ reduce the further disruption for the child which may result where a return order is made after a settled period abroad;

▪ prevent or limit any advantage to the abductor gained by the passage of time.

Without derogating from the importance of speed as a key operating principle, a Central Authority or its intermediary needs to exercise some discretion in resolving any conflict between taking action promptly or speedily, and allowing time to negotiate an amicable resolution of the matter or a voluntary return. *See* Chapter 4.12 for a discussion of voluntary return issues.

1.6 Transparency

Throughout the Hague application process, there should be transparency in both legal process and administrative procedure.

---

[16] Conclusion IV, First Special Commission.

Transparency in the administrative procedure requires that interested parties have access to information about those procedures. The information may be published on a website, or in a brochure, or provided by the Central Authority.

Central Authorities should provide clear information about their country's processes and procedures for the benefit of the parties, other Central Authorities, courts and other interested parties.

Transparency of process as a means of building trust and confidence should not be underestimated.

1.7 Progressive implementation

It is desirable that Central Authorities, and their States, acknowledge the value of the concept of "progressive implementation" of the Convention. All Central Authorities have had to review and revise their early procedures, as they gained more practical experience with the Convention, and obtained more information about practices in other countries. Many countries have also amended their initial implementing legislation in the light of changing interpretations and practices since 1980.

This evolution in practices and procedures contributes to more effective ways to implement the Convention and achieve its objectives. Recognition of progressive implementation as a key operating principle ensures that all Central Authorities, both established and developing, and their Contracting States, will take steps whenever possible to improve the operation of the Convention in their respective countries.

2.   SUMMARY: ESTABLISHING AND CONSOLIDATING THE CENTRAL AUTHORITY

2.1   Why?

2.1.1   The designation and establishment of a Central Authority is an obligation of the Convention under Article 6

2.1.2   Designation of "central" Central Authorities for Federal States is necessary

2.2   When?

2.2.1   The Central Authority should be designated at the time of ratification or accession to the Convention

2.2.2   The Central Authority must be established and ready to send and receive applications at the time the Convention enters into force for the Contracting State

2.3   Where?

2.3.1   The Central Authority is a position or office created to carry out the obligations and functions of the Convention

2.3.2   The Office of the Central Authority should have a connection with the subject matter of the Convention

2.3.3   The Office of the Central Authority should have strong links to the internal justice and welfare system

2.4   Who?

The personnel or staff of the Central Authority should be:

2.4.1   Sufficient in numbers to cope with the workload

2.4.2   Properly qualified and trained to understand the requirements of the Convention

2.4.3   Properly qualified and trained to understand how the Convention operates within their domestic legal and administrative framework

2.4.4   Of a suitable temperament to work co-operatively with foreign agencies and with children and parents in distress

2.4.5   Committed to achieving the goals of the Convention

2.4.6   Competent in relevant foreign language skills

2.4.7   Personnel who will remain for a reasonable period of time in their positions

2.5   What?

2.5.1   Equipment and materials for all Central Authorities.

The minimum level of essential equipment and materials includes:

- telephone

- fax machine

- stationery

- computer/word processor or typewriter

- copy of the Convention

- translation of the Convention into the national language

- copy of applicable implementing legislation or procedures

- copy of the Explanatory Report to the Convention by Elisa Pérez-Vera

- list of lawyers or administrative officials who are able to represent the applicant in any Convention proceedings

- written procedures for handling Convention applications

- list of qualified translators to translate applications

- the Guide to Good Practice

- full contact details for all other Central Authorities

- a register for maintenance of statistics

2.5.2   Equipment and materials in well-resourced Central Authorities

A well resourced Central Authority will have, in addition to the items listed above:

- email facilities

- internet access

- library/collection of Convention literature

- materials for education programmes

- office procedures manual for Convention applications

- arrangements through Interpol, local police or Central Authority personnel on call, to provide 24 hour contact

- strategic plan for twinning arrangements

- electronic case management system

2. ESTABLISHING AND CONSOLIDATING THE CENTRAL AUTHORITY

2.1 Why?

2.1.1 Designation and establishment of the Central Authority

The designation of a Central Authority is an essential Convention obligation under Article 6. Of equal importance is ensuring that the designated Central Authority is established with adequate personnel and resources to deal with abduction applications.

The designation and establishment of a Central Authority is absolutely vital for the effective implementation of the Convention. The importance of these steps cannot be over-emphasised. *See also* Guide to Good Practice, Part II - Implementing Measures, at Chapter 4.

The entire framework of the Convention is built upon the co-operation of Central Authorities. The critical first steps to secure the return of an abducted child - to send or receive an application – cannot easily be taken without a Central Authority.[17]

It has been a significant cause for concern that some countries have ratified or acceded to the Convention without, at the same time, designating a Central Authority. Other States have designated a Central Authority but failed to provide any personnel or resources necessary to enable the Authority to carry out its functions. In either case, the inability to send or receive applications has the potential to seriously damage a child's interests, and the interests of the left-behind parent. The result will be frustration and anger on the part of the individuals involved and a possible source of friction between the States concerned. Confidence in the functioning of the Convention is also undermined.

2.1.2 Designation of "central" Central Authorities for Federal States

Federal States are free to appoint more than one Central Authority, but where this is done, it is a Convention obligation under Article 6 to designate a "central" Central Authority to which applications should be addressed for transmission to the appropriate Central Authority.

Federal States must ensure that their designation of a "central" Central Authority is absolutely clear at the time of ratification or accession. The different roles of their "central" Central Authority and their state, regional or provincial Central Authorities must also be made very clear to other Contracting States and Central Authorities.

---

[17] Article 29 permits a person, institution or body to apply directly to a Contracting State.

2.2 When?

2.2.1 Designated at the time of ratification or accession

The Central Authority should be designated at the time of ratification or accession to the Convention.

2.2.2 Established at time of entry into force

The Central Authority must be established and ready to send and receive applications at the time the Convention enters into force for the Contracting State.

Other countries have an expectation that as soon as the Convention enters into force for a new country, it should be possible to send applications to secure the return of abducted children through co-operation with the designated Central Authority.

Ideally it should be apparent well before ratification or accession takes place where the position or office of Central Authority will be located. The designated office and its personnel should then be involved in advising the appropriate officials of its resource requirements (personnel and equipment), as well as undertaking preliminary staff training and planning its procedures for sending and receiving applications.

2.3 Where?

2.3.1 A position or office

The Central Authority is a position or office created to carry out the obligations and functions set out in the Convention. The Convention does not require a Central Authority to be established by legislation. This depends on the requirements of each legal system. Establishment by administrative decree may be sufficient.

2.3.2 Office of the Central Authority should have a connection with the subject matter of the Convention

The best location for the office of Central Authority in each country will be in an office which has functions that are closely related to the subject matter of the Convention. Whatever location is chosen, experience suggests that the policy and Central Authority functions for the Convention should be closely linked.

Usually the Central Authority is established in a government authority such as a ministry of justice, a ministry of child and family issues, or a ministry of foreign affairs. Alternatively, a non-government organisation with similar responsibilities for children could be appointed.[18]

---

[18] The National Center for Missing and Exploited Children (NCMEC) in the USA and Reunite in the UK are examples of non-government organisations which carry out functions for or on behalf of their Central Authorities. NCMEC acts under the direction of the US Central Authority to perform operation functions with respect to Hague Convention applications seeking return of or access to children in the United States. Reunite's functions include advising parents, educating

The best location of the position or office will also depend on a number of other factors, including the extent of the powers and functions vested in it by the Contracting State.

For example, the Central Authority might simply act as a "clearing-house", sending applications on to be dealt with by private lawyers, or by other government or non-government bodies or individuals. Central Authorities operating with a low level of involvement in cases must ensure that they are nevertheless monitoring applications sufficiently closely so as to be able to fulfil their Convention obligations as Central Authority.

Alternatively, the Central Authority may be fully involved in all stages of the administrative and legal process, with a wide network of agencies to assist in carrying out Convention-related functions.

2.3.3 *Strong links to the internal justice and welfare system*

The Central Authority should have strong links to the justice and welfare system of the Contracting State. The need for co-operation between the Central Authority, the courts, the legal profession, the police and social welfare professionals make these links essential for the effective operation of the Convention. *See also* Chapter 1.2.4: "Improving co-operation by eliminating obstacles to the application of the Convention".

2.4   Who?

2.4.1 *Sufficient numbers to cope with the workload*

The number of cases in each Contracting State will vary considerably, depending on such factors as population size, geography, and mobility of the population.[19] Socio-demographic factors such as the number of separations and divorces in a State may also be reflected in the number of abductions. In each of the largest volume Central Authorities, personnel functions vary. In some authorities, personnel may work only on child abduction cases, while in others they work on a variety of matters. In small volume States, there may only be one person dealing with child abduction cases and a range of other tasks.

2.4.2 *Proper qualifications and training to understand the requirements of the Convention*

If there is no legal expert working in the Central Authority, there should be arrangements in place for access to legal advice when necessary.

Personnel should be properly prepared so that they can:

- check applications to ensure they meet the requirements of the Convention;

- advise potential clients about assistance available from the Convention.

---

parents and professionals about the Convention, lobbying government, organising conferences, responding to media enquiries about the Convention. The Central Authority for England and Wales provides some funding to Reunite for these functions.

[19] In 1999, the USA had 466 applications; UK had 357; Canada 103; Australia 172; Bermuda had 0.

2.4.3 Proper qualifications and training to understand how the Convention operates within their domestic legal and administrative framework

Personnel should have sufficient understanding of how the Convention operates in their country in order to:

- advise applicants or other Central Authorities how an application will proceed through the legal system of the requested country;

- advise applicants of any steps they must take independently in the requested country;

- obtain legal advice when needed on Convention issues or applications;

- inform their managers or government on ways to overcome obstacles to, or improve the implementation of the Convention in their country;

- liaise with relevant national agencies such as police and child welfare agencies on ways to overcome obstacles to, or improve the implementation of the Convention in their country;

- form links, if possible, with NGOs and national or regional law associations.

Beyond these general functions, Central Authority personnel are not expected to act as legal advisers to applicants or respondents.

2.4.4 Suitable temperament to work co-operatively with foreign agencies and distressed children and parents

To work co-operatively with foreign agencies and distressed people requires:

- sensitivity to cultural and linguistic differences;

- patience with foreign personnel who speak a different language;

- patience and empathy with emotionally volatile people suffering the trauma of child abduction.

2.4.5 Commitment to achieving the goals of the Convention

If personnel are committed to achieving the goals of the Convention, they will:

- be professional and objective in dealing with applications;

- not be influenced by issues of nationalism, gender bias, class or racial prejudice;

- do their utmost to secure the return of abducted children;

- do their utmost to carry out fully the obligations of Article 7.

2.4.6 Competence in relevant foreign language skills

Competency in relevant foreign language skills improves communication with other Central Authorities and builds co-operative and productive relationships. There have been noticeable benefits reported from Central Authorities which have employed caseworkers who are fluent in the languages of their high volume Convention partners.

A minimum standard for Central Authority good practice is that there should be personnel who are competent in French and English as the working languages of the Convention.

2.4.7 Personnel who will remain for a reasonable period of time in their positions

Continuity with personnel:

- creates stability for the Central Authority;

- allows an accumulation of knowledge and experience to be passed on to others in training;

- is conducive to building good relationships with other Central Authorities over a period of time.

The exchange of personnel between Central Authorities of various jurisdictions should be encouraged where it is feasible, to foster co-operation and improve understanding of different legal and administrative systems.

2.5 What?

2.5.1 Equipment and materials for all Central Authorities

A properly resourced Central Authority office must have, at the very minimum, the following materials or equipment in good working order:

- telephone;

- fax machine;

- stationery;

- computer/word processor (or typewriter);

- copy of the Convention in the original French and English versions;

- official translation of the Convention in the national language;

- copy of implementing legislation or procedures;

- copy of the Explanatory Report to the Convention by Elisa Pérez-Vera (available in English, French and Spanish on the Hague Conference website);

- details (name, address, phone, fax and email) of legal counsel or pro bono lawyers or administrative officials who are able to represent the applicant in any judicial or administrative proceedings for return of children;

- written procedures for handling Convention applications, for receiving and sending correspondence and to avoid loss or misplacement of files;

- list of qualified translators to translate applications;

- copy of the Guide to Good Practice;

- full contact details for all other Central Authorities, either in hard copy or via Internet access on the Hague Conference website;

- register for the maintenance of statistics. *See* Chapter 6.1 for details.

Fax machines

Avoid having the same number or line for the telephone and the fax machine. Fax machines should be left switched on 24 hours a day to receive messages from countries in different time zones.

2.5.2 Equipment and materials in well-resourced Central Authorities

A well resourced Central Authority office may have the following equipment and materials, in addition to the essential items above:

- email facilities;

- internet access;

- library/collection of Convention literature;

- education programme or materials for the general public, government officials, lawyers, and judges;

- an office manual describing procedures for Convention applications;

- arrangements through Interpol, local police or Central Authority personnel on call, to provide 24 hour contact;

- strategic plan for twinning arrangements with a developing Central Authority;

- an electronic case management system.

Office procedures manual

To implement the objects of the Convention as expeditiously as possible, Central Authorities must be guided by the key operating principles in all matters (resources and powers, co-operation, communication, consistency, expeditious procedures, transparency and progressive implementation). To be able to do this, they should prepare an office manual of established procedures.

Administrative and legal procedures must be organised to meet the time objectives of the Convention. In summary, the office procedures manual may include descriptions of:

- established office procedures for receiving, processing and sending applications;

- clear timeframes or timescales for each stage of the process;

- well-organised office procedures for responding to requests for information and monitoring progress of applications;

- established arrangements for contact or networks with other domestic agencies and authorities to assist in locating a child;

- established arrangements to provide or facilitate the provision of legal representation for applicants;

- established procedures to arrange the safe return of a child;

- training programme for new personnel.

24 hour contact

Arrangements should be made with Interpol, local police or Central Authority personnel "on call" to have 24 hour contacts in child abduction matters. These arrangements are necessary not just for emergencies, but also because of the global operation of the Convention. Globally, different time zones and hemispheres mean that sunrise in one part of the world means sunset in another.[20]

Most Central Authorities are in government offices and (most) personnel work normal office hours. In some Contracting States, Interpol, and national and local police are well informed about child abduction matters and they have the after hours contact details of Central Authority personnel. Such personnel are "on call" at any time for real emergencies. Fortunately, 24 hour fax and email access is sufficient for the majority of cases. The important issue is to establish a "chain of communication" so that the relevant personnel can be reached after hours in emergencies.

Email contact has proved to be a wonderful bridge across time zones, and also as a means to improve personal contact between Central Authority personnel in different countries. However, it does have some disadvantages: lack of security or confidentiality and messages may remain unread if the addressee is unexpectedly absent (*see* Chapter 1.3.3).

Twinning arrangements

---

[20] UNDCP Informal Expert Working Group Report on Mutual Legal Assistance Casework Best Practice, Vienna, 3-7 December 2001, p. 8.

A "twinning" arrangement could occur if a developing Central Authority sought assistance from an experienced Central Authority which was willing to provide extra assistance. The latter could then provide training, advice, materials, and other guidance. The arrangement could extend to the donation of equipment and may foster visits or exchanges of administrative and judicial officers. This issue is discussed in more detail in Chapter 6.5.

3. SUMMARY: ABDUCTION APPLICATIONS (OUTGOING): ROLE OF THE REQUESTING CENTRAL AUTHORITY

OUTLINE OF PROCEDURES

Preparing and sending applications

3.1   Obtain information about procedures in the requested country

3.2   Check that the application is complete and in an acceptable form for the requested country

3.3   Check that the application satisfies Convention requirements

3.4   Discuss the operation of the Convention with the applicant

3.5   Provide information about relevant laws

3.6   Ensure all essential supporting documents are included

3.7   Provide a translation of the application and all essential documents

3.8   Ensure the application is sent to the correct postal address or fax number or email address of the requested Central Authority

3.9   Send the original application by priority mail, and fax or email an advance copy of the application

3.10 If the application is very urgent, explain the reasons for the urgency

Assisting and responding to the requested Central Authority

3.11 If the requested Central Authority requires additional information, ensure that all the information is provided promptly

3.12 Advise the requested Central Authority if there are difficulties in meeting their deadlines

3.13 Be reasonable about requests for follow-up information

3.14 Monitor progress of the application

3.15 Assist the applicant to obtain an Article 15 declaration or determination if necessary

Procedures following return order

3.16 Additional enforcement action is sometimes needed in particular countries

3.17 Be aware of the appeals process in the requested country

3.18 Co-operate with the requested Central Authority to facilitate a safe return of the child, and where necessary, the accompanying parent

3.19 Provide requested Central Authority with confirmation of the return of the child

3.20 Verify agreed arrangements with the appropriate protection and welfare authorities in the requesting country are in place when the child returns

3.21 If conditions were imposed or undertakings given with the return order, take whatever steps are appropriate within the limits of the Central Authority's powers, to ensure that the conditions are met or the undertakings are fulfilled

3. ABDUCTION APPLICATIONS (OUTGOING): ROLE OF THE REQUESTING CENTRAL AUTHORITY

OUTLINE OF PROCEDURES

3.1 Obtain information about procedures in requested country

As a routine measure, obtain the details of abduction procedures in the requested Central Authority from their website, brochure or flyer.[21] This will save time in preparing and checking applications, it will prevent delays caused by incomplete applications, and avoid unnecessary requests to the Central Authority for information about their procedures. In Federal States or States with more than one Central Authority, the different procedures or requirements in each of their states, provinces or regions should be made known.

If information about procedures in the requested country is available, they can then be explained to an applicant at the outset, and will usually satisfy the applicant that his/her application is proceeding normally.

It is not advisable to delay sending an application if procedural information is not readily available.

3.2 Check that the application is complete and in an acceptable form for the requested country

The application to be sent should:

- be legible, preferably typed not hand-written[22]

- be clearly expressed and comprehensible

- contain all essential information to identify and locate the child

- be in an appropriate form, acceptable to the requested country. It is recommended that the model form be used (*see* Chapter 1.4.1)

- contain adequate supporting documentation

- include documents or information specifically required by the legal or administrative system of the requested country

Article 8 imposes an obligation on the requesting Central Authority to ensure that the application contains information about:

- the applicant;

- the child;

---

[21] Conclusion 1.8, Fourth Special Commission.
[22] The courts of some countries will not accept hand-written applications. These countries must make their requirements clear in their procedural information.

- the abductor;

- the legal and factual grounds on which the applicant's claim for return of the child is based;

- all available information about the location of the child, in particular, where and with whom the child is living or possibly hiding.

In some countries, the Central Authority will retype a handwritten application to make it legible and acceptable in the requested country. At the same time, deficiencies in the application are also rectified. The typed application is then returned to the applicant for signing. Some Central Authorities have the power to appoint a lawyer to assist an applicant to prepare a request for return.[23]

If an application simply has to be re-typed, it may be possible to attach the original application to the typed application instead of re-signing.

The requesting Central Authority should ensure that each application is accompanied by a sufficient statement of the legal and factual basis on which the application rests, in particular concerning the matters of the habitual residence of the child, rights of custody and the exercise of those rights, as well as detailed information on location of the child.[24]

Some Central Authorities will directly or indirectly assist an applicant to prepare a request for return, at the same time ensuring that the application is complete and all essential documents are attached.[25]

Failure to provide essential information in the application will inevitably lead to delays which may:

- prejudice the applicant's prospects of obtaining a successful return;

- frustrate and anger the applicant who then becomes abusive to Central Authority personnel; and

- waste the time of the requested Central Authority.

3.3 Check that the application satisfies Convention requirements

The requirements of the Convention are explained in Chapter 4.5. A sample checklist is at Appendix 3.5.

Central Authorities should carefully scrutinise outgoing applications to ensure they come within the Convention. Otherwise the application may be rejected by the requested Central Authority according to Article 27.

It may be necessary to provide additional supporting documentation to persuade the requested Central Authority that the application should be accepted.

Central Authorities must accept applications in good faith. At the same time, requesting Central Authorities should ensure that their applicants provide adequate documentation

---

[23] *For example*, New Zealand.
[24] Conclusion 1.6, Fourth Special Commission.
[25] Austria, Australia, Belgium, Ireland, South Africa.

to support their request for return. Experience has shown that applicants sometimes make claims that are quickly and convincingly rebutted once the taking parent has filed his/her response to the return application.

3.4 Discuss the operation of the Convention with the applicant

Whenever possible, Central Authorities should discuss with applicants the aims and operation of the Convention, and the possible results of the application. This will assist the applicant to have realistic expectations for his/her application.

Confidentiality of communications is important. The applicant should be aware that confidentiality of personal information cannot always be guaranteed in the requested country's administrative and legal procedures, particularly when email communications are being used.

3.5 Provide information about the relevant laws of the requesting country

Article 7(e) of the Convention requires Central Authorities to take all appropriate measures to provide information about the laws of their country in connection with the application of the Convention. Central Authorities should, as a routine procedure, ensure that a copy of their laws relating to the applicant's rights of custody is provided with every application.

This practice will save time when the requested Central Authority considers whether the application comes within the Convention. It will avoid future delays in the legal proceedings if information about the relevant laws is provided for the court or tribunal at the time of filing the application for return.

Some Central Authorities provide the relevant laws in the original language, and a translation into English or French, or the language of the requested country.

Some Central Authorities have adopted the helpful practice of attaching to each application a comprehensive covering letter which:

- describes the relevant laws;

- explains the applicant's rights of custody;

- summarises the important aspects of the application.[26]

3.6 Ensure all essential supporting documents are included

Supporting documents may include:

- a copy of laws relating to the applicant's rights of custody;

- an affidavit or sworn statement explaining the applicant's rights of custody (especially where this is not clear from the laws themselves);

---

[26] An example of the Australian covering letter is at Appendix 4.3.

- documentary evidence of particular claims made *e.g.* court orders concerning rights of custody;

- photographs of the child and abductor;

- documents to satisfy specific requirements of the requested country;

- written authorisation where required in accordance with Article 28.

Requesting Central Authorities should ensure that applications are not excessively long, or accompanied by large amounts of irrelevant material. *See* sample letter of advice to applicant or applicant's lawyer at Appendix 4.4.

A checklist of general Convention requirements as well as country specific requirements may assist personnel responsible for checking outgoing applications. *See* Sample Checklist at Appendix 3.6.

3.7 Provide a translation of the application and all essential documents

Translations should be in the language of the requested country, and if this is not feasible,[27] in French or English. Check if the requested country has made a reservation objecting to the use of either French or English, in accordance with Article 24.

Although the Central Authority is obliged under Article 24 to accept an application in French or English where translation into the language of the requested country is not feasible, the reality is that courts and tribunals may be less receptive to foreign language documents. In all language issues, the spirit of co-operation that underpins the Convention should be remembered.

Sometimes applications are sent with translations of such poor quality that the application is incomprehensible. Although it may be expensive, it is preferable to use a qualified translator for applications. Delays are inevitable, or rejection may follow, if the application is incomprehensible to the requested Central Authority.

Some Central Authorities pay for the cost of translations for their applicants. In some countries, legal aid for an eligible applicant will also cover the cost of translations.[28]

3.8 Ensure the application is sent to the correct address

Check the Hague Conference website for the current address of the requested Central Authority. If there are any difficulties in sending the application, for example, if the Central Authority cannot be contacted, inform the Permanent Bureau immediately.

3.9 Send the application by priority mail, and by fax or email

Applications should, if possible, be sent to the requested Central Authority by a secure mail system (or equivalent) to ensure their safe arrival. If there are any concerns about

---

[27] "Not feasible" could mean, for example, that there is no translator for the language in question in the requesting country.
[28] *For example*, Israel.

the reliability of the mail system in the requested country, or if there are communication problems with the requested Central Authority, it may be possible to send applications via diplomatic channel, or by diplomatic bag with the agreement of the relevant embassies. Send the original application by priority mail, and fax or email an advance copy of the application.

3.10 Urgent applications

If the application is very urgent or the 12 month deadline for a mandatory return is imminent, inform the requested Central Authority of the reasons for the urgency. The requested country may accept the application in the original language in order to prepare or file a petition for return, provided the translation will be sent as soon as possible.

3.11 Providing additional information

If the requested Central Authority requires additional information, ensure that all the information is provided promptly, or as soon as possible.

Applicants who prepare their own applications often have difficulty understanding what documents or information they have to produce for the foreign court. Central Authorities should, where possible, provide guidance and assistance for their own applicants.

3.12 Advise the requested Central Authority if there are difficulties in meeting their deadlines

If deadlines are set for sending/receiving information, advise the requested Central Authority if there are difficulties in meeting their deadlines. Deadlines for filing documents or providing evidence are usually set by courts or tribunals. However, it may be possible to get an extension of the deadline. Failure to meet deadlines for providing information or documents may result in the non-return of the child.

3.13 Be reasonable about requests for follow-up information

Central Authorities should be reasonable about requests for follow-up information. All Central Authority personnel seem to be overworked and under constant pressure. Avoid creating additional work for the requested Central Authority.

In the early stages of a return request, it is reasonable to expect the requested Central Authority (or, for later steps, its intermediary) to:

- acknowledge receipt;

- advise the requesting Central Authority if additional information is required;

- advise of the appointment of a lawyer (or steps being taken to find a lawyer) for the applicant;

- advise of the dates for filing documents in court and commencement of legal proceedings;

- notify Central Authority if the applicant's attendance is required at the court hearing (*see also* Chapter 3.16);

- notify Central Authority of the date for any legal proceedings, including appeals.

Requesting Central Authorities are often under pressure from applicants (usually left-behind parents) to provide daily reports of progress. This pressure should be resisted, where it is unreasonable.

Article 11 states that where a requested court or administrative authority has not made a decision within six weeks from the commencement of proceedings, the requesting Central Authority is entitled to ask for an explanation for the delay.

It should be recognised that the limitations on some Central Authorities to take certain actions is not a lack of co-operation but a lack of power to act.

3.14 Monitor progress of the application

If the requested Central Authority has not provided follow-up information as suggested above, the requesting authority is entitled to make regular requests for this information. *See also* Chapter 4.18 for a discussion of the requested Central Authority's monitoring responsibilities.

If the applicant and the lawyer representing the applicant are communicating directly about the application, ensure that the requesting Central Authority is kept informed of developments.

3.15 Article 15 declaration or determination

The authorities in the requesting country may be asked to provide a declaration or determination in accordance with Article 15 that the removal was wrongful. Not every country is able to provide this declaration or determination, but for those countries that can provide it, the declaration may be made by the court, the Central Authority or other authority.

Central Authorities are obliged under Article 15 to assist applicants to obtain a decision or determination, as far as practicable.

3.16 Further proceedings for enforcement of a return order

In some countries,[29] after a return order is made, the applicant has to initiate further legal proceedings to have the order enforced. Many requesting countries have not been aware of the need for this additional step, through lack of information from the requested country.

Make every effort to ensure that the procedures of the requested country are understood, to avoid any disadvantage to the applicant as a result of poor communication.

---

[29] Finland, Austria, the Czech Republic and Greece are known to have this requirement.

3.17 Appeals

The Central Authority should be aware of the appeals procedure in the requested country. When a parent is advised of the non-return of the child, their first question will often be about whether and how to appeal the decision.

If a requested court refuses to order a return, make every effort to ensure that the applicant is aware of the rights of appeal available to the applicant, and any action, legal or administrative, that the applicant needs to take to safeguard those rights. The Central Authority should advise applicants of any strict deadlines for appeal and, to the extent appropriate and feasible, assist applicants in meeting such deadlines.

3.18 Co-operate with requested Central Authority to facilitate a safe return

The role of the Central Authorities (requested and requesting) in securing the safe return of the child was discussed in considerable detail at previous Special Commissions, in particular, the Special Commissions of 1997 and 2001.

To the extent permitted by the powers of their Central Authority and by the legal and social welfare systems of their country, Contracting States accept that Central Authorities have an obligation under Article 7(h) to ensure appropriate child protection bodies are alerted so they may act to protect the welfare of children upon return in certain cases where their safety is at issue until the jurisdiction of the appropriate court has been effectively invoked.[30]

It is recognised that, in most cases, a consideration of the child's best interests requires that both parents have the opportunity to participate and be heard in custody proceedings. Central Authorities should therefore co-operate to the fullest extent possible to provide information in respect of legal, financial, protection and other resources in the requesting State, and facilitate timely contact with these bodies in appropriate cases.

The measures which may be taken in fulfilment of the obligation under Article 7(h) to take or cause to be taken an action to protect the welfare of children may include, for example:

- alerting the appropriate protection agencies or judicial authorities in the requesting State of the return of a child who may be in danger;

- advising the requested State, upon request, of the protective measures and services available in the requesting State to secure the safe return of a particular child;

- encouraging the use of Article 21 of the Convention to secure the effective exercise of access or visitation rights.

It is recognised that for the purposes of return, the protection of the child may also sometimes require steps to be taken to protect an accompanying parent.[31]

---

[30] Conclusion 1.13, Fourth Special Commission.
[31] Conclusion 1.13, Fourth Special Commission.

In 1993, the Special Commission concluded that: "Practical arrangements for the safe return of children should be under contemplation from the commencement of the application".[32]

The levels of assistance provided by Central Authorities in this area differ considerably, depending on the powers and resources of each Central Authority. Some of the practices utilised by various Central Authorities are listed in Appendix 5.2.

A related issue for protection on return, and return generally, is the procedure for cases in which the applicant has moved to another country. The Convention is silent on this issue. While some countries do permit a return to a country other than to the habitual residence, other countries do not. This is an area where there needs to be co-operation between the Central Authorities or other authorities concerned.

3.19 Provide confirmation of return

If possible, inform the requested Central Authority when the child has returned. It appears that many Central Authorities have no procedures in place to confirm the return of a child. Indeed, many Central Authorities may find it impossible to request or obtain such information.

While there is no Convention obligation to confirm a child's return, it is good practice to do so, if at all possible. It is desirable for the Central Authorities concerned to know that the Convention process has concluded with the actual return of the child, rather than simply a court order for return.[33]

3.20 Verify agreed protection arrangements are in place when the child returns

If the requesting Central Authority has assisted in making arrangements with the appropriate protection and welfare authorities for the returning child (and parent), verify that these arrangements are in place when the child returns.

In some countries, a social worker specialising in child protection matters is employed in the Central Authority to deal with issues concerning the safe return of the child to the requesting country. The social worker also counsels distressed parents.[34]

Within the limits of the Central Authority's powers, assist with any arrangements to bring the matter before the local courts as quickly as possible, for a determination on the interim arrangements for the child in the habitual residence country. It is recognized that the Central Authority's role in matters relating to custody determinations may be extremely limited or non-existent.

---

[32] Conclusion 4, Second Special Commission.
[33] There is a growing academic and judicial interest in knowing what happens in the requesting country after a child returns: are there further custody proceedings? which parent obtains custody? are the child and abductor permitted to relocate to another country? Information about current research may be obtained from the Permanent Bureau.
[34] France.

3.21 Take any appropriate steps to ensure that conditions are met or undertakings are fulfilled

If conditions were imposed or undertakings given with the return order, take whatever steps are appropriate within the limits of the Central Authority's powers, so that the conditions are met or the undertakings are fulfilled. It is recognised that the Central Authority's role in matters of conditions or undertakings may be extremely limited or non-existent.

4.   SUMMARY: ABDUCTION APPLICATIONS (INCOMING): ROLE OF THE REQUESTED CENTRAL AUTHORITY

OUTLINE OF PROCEDURES

Receiving and acknowledging applications

4.1   Observe internal or external timeframes

4.2   Applications may be received by mail or by fax or email

4.3   Register the receipt of the application on an internal register

4.4   Acknowledge receipt of the application

4.5   Check the application to ensure Convention requirements are satisfied

4.6   If additional information or documents are required, advise the requesting Central Authority in the acknowledgement letter/email or in a follow-up letter/email

4.7   If the application is very urgent, or if the 12 month deadline for a mandatory return is imminent, make every effort to expedite matters more quickly than usual

4.8   Inform the court of the Article 16 limitations on custody hearings

4.9   If the application will not be accepted, inform the requesting Central Authority of reasons

Actions following acceptance of applications

4.10   Locate the child and confirm that he/she is actually in the requested country

4.11   If the child is not located, return the application; if the child has moved to another territory, forward the application as appropriate

4.12   If the application meets the Convention requirements, consider if a voluntary return is appropriate and feasible

4.13   Arrange legal representation for the applicant or assist the applicant to obtain legal representation

4.14   Provide the requesting Central Authority with follow-up information about action taken on behalf of the applicant

4.15   Take steps to prevent further harm to the child or prejudice to interested parties

4.16   Initiate or facilitate legal proceedings. Legal proceedings may be commenced even if a voluntary return is contemplated

4.17   Applicants should not be required to attend court hearings in the requested country, unless it is absolutely essential and the court requires it

4.18   Monitor progress of the application

4.19   Inform requesting Central Authority as soon as a court decision is known

4.20   Ensure that the requesting Central Authority or the applicant is aware of his/her rights of appeal

Practical arrangements for the return of the child

4.21   Consider the practical arrangements for return of the child. These arrangements should be under consideration well before a return order is made

4.22   If conditions or undertakings are to be included in the return order, the Central Authority should be consulted by the applicant's lawyer about the reasonableness of the conditions or undertakings

4.23   If a return is to be ordered, the Central Authority may be consulted on any issues or concerns about the safe return of the child or parent

4.24   Ensure that the abductor who wishes to return with the child is provided with information about services or assistance available in the requesting country

4.25   Assistance with enforcement of a return order may be sought from police or other agencies

4.26   Get confirmation from the requesting country that the child (and parent) has (have) returned

4.27   Maximise opportunities to inform the professions about the principles and procedures of the Hague Convention

4. ABDUCTION APPLICATIONS (INCOMING): ROLE OF THE REQUESTED CENTRAL AUTHORITY

OUTLINE OF PROCEDURES

This chapter attempts to outline the main procedures to be followed in handling an application, from receipt to conclusion. While each country will have particular procedures adapted to its system of law and administration, the general procedures described here for the most part follow the requirements and obligations of the Convention, and must therefore be carried out in the manner appropriate, and to the extent possible, in each country.

4.1 Observe internal or external timeframes

The Central Authority's administrative procedures for handling applications should set timeframes or timescales by which each stage of the process is to be completed. For example, one Central Authority has a target of referring new applications to a lawyer within 24 hours in 85% of cases.

The procedures should also describe at what point and in what way the Central Authority will act if timeframes are exceeded.

In some Contracting States the implementing legislation sets time limits for various stages of the legal proceedings which also impact on the Central Authority.[35]

Adherence to these timeframes is essential for good practice. How that is achieved is a matter for each Central Authority to determine.

4.2 Receiving applications by mail or by fax or email

Applications should, if possible, be sent to the requested Central Authority by a secure mail system (or equivalent) to ensure their safe arrival. If there are any concerns about the reliability of the mail system in the requested country, it may be possible to send applications through the diplomatic bag, with the agreement of the relevant embassies.

Some Central Authorities routinely fax the application and mail the original. This usually guarantees that a copy of the application is received and allows the requested Central Authority extra time to complete its preliminary administrative procedures, and to arrange or facilitate legal representation for the applicant. To encourage speed, there is no reason that a requested Central Authority should not act on the basis of faxed documents to:

- register receipt (Chapter 4.3)

- acknowledge receipt (Chapter 4.4)

- check that the application meets Convention requirements (Chapter 4.5)

- request additional information (Chapter 4.6)

---

[35] Scotland, Australia.

- begin the process to locate the child (Chapter 4.10)

It is recognised that in most countries, the original application (not the fax) is essential to file a petition in court. *See also* Chapter 4.7 for urgent applications.

4.3 Register the receipt of the application

Applications received should be registered promptly on an internal electronic or manual register as a record of receipt and for future monitoring. The register should be part of the administrative procedures developed by the Central Authority for handling all applications. The register and related procedures should be used as a basis for tracking or monitoring the progress of applications.

4.4 Acknowledge receipt of the application

Acknowledge receipt of applications promptly. It is very disturbing for a requesting Central Authority to receive no acknowledgement or no reply to a request for return. Failure to acknowledge or reply will result in even more correspondence from the requesting authority.

A simple procedure should be developed to acknowledge receipt of applications. For example, the quickest procedure is probably to send an email message of acknowledgement. Central Authorities without email could use a standard one (1) page form or letter with appropriate boxes to tick to indicate receipt of the application, and the proposed next steps. This form can be faxed to the requesting Central Authority soon after the requested Central Authority receives the application. The office timeframe for sending acknowledgements should be adhered to (*see* 4.1 above).

A sample form is at Appendix 3.3.

A step-by-step guide to the entire legal and administrative process in handling an application would be helpful. It is possible that such a guide could be routinely attached to an acknowledgment of receipt of a request for return.

4.5 Check that the application appears to come within the Convention

Checking and processing of applications should be done quickly. If the application appears, on the face of the documents, to come within the Convention, the application should be accepted. *See also* Chapter 4.9 "Reasons for refusing to accept an application".

Issues such as rights of custody, habitual residence, whether the child is settled in the country of refuge, or is at grave risk of harm, are ultimately issues for determination by a court or tribunal, not the Central Authority.

The basic requirements to be satisfied are set out in Articles 3 and 4. These are:

- the child was removed to or retained in the State of the requested Central Authority;

- the applicant had custody rights that were breached by removal/retention;

- the applicant was actually exercising such custody rights at the time of the removal/retention;

- the child was habitually resident in a Convention country at the time of the removal or retention; and

- the child is not yet 16.

A checklist of Convention requirements will expedite the initial checking process. *See* sample checklist in Appendix 3.4.

Central Authorities have complained about:

- inordinate delays in relation to the processing of applications;

- undue and unnecessary formality with respect to documentation.[36]

Take steps and adopt procedures which avoid these obstacles to the Convention.

4.6 Requesting additional information or documents

If a requested country has specific requirements for information or documents, beyond what is stated in the model form, then the Central Authority has a responsibility to make those requirements known to other requesting authorities. The website, brochure or flyer is a convenient tool to disseminate this information.

If additional information or documents are required, advise the requesting Central Authority in the acknowledgement letter/email or in a follow-up letter/email. The documents most commonly omitted from applications are evidence of the applicant's rights of custody, and evidence of the laws relating to the applicant's rights of custody. *See* a sample letter at Appendix 4.1.

In the early stages, Central Authorities should only request sufficient additional information to be satisfied that the application comes within the Convention. Usually, the applicant's legal representative, or the court, requires additional information after the abductor has filed his/her response to the return petition. The Central Authority should not delay processing the application to obtain information that may or may not be needed later in legal proceedings.

A requested Central Authority should not be criticised for failure to act promptly if the application for return is incomplete. At the same time, Central Authorities must publicise or make known their specific legal and administrative requirements for return requests. In accordance with the principles of good communication and good co-operation, it will sometimes be necessary to explain to requesting Central Authorities the policy or practical reasons behind a country's specific legal or administrative requirements.

4.7 Urgent applications

If the application is very urgent, or if the 12 month deadline for a mandatory return is imminent, make every effort to expedite matters more quickly than usual. Do not insist

---

[36] Questionnaires completed for Fourth Special Commission.

on excessively complex or bureaucratic procedures. In some countries, courts permit faxed documents rather than originals to be filed in urgent cases, provided originals will be produced at a later date.[37]

No legalisation of documents is required under this Convention. This is clearly stated in Article 23.

The correct contact details for the Central Authority and its personnel are vital to ensure that days are not wasted attempting to fax or phone a Central Authority that has changed its numbers. In such situations, an urgent application may then have to be sent by post, and this may be too late for a successful return.

4.8 Inform the court of Article 16 limitations on custody hearings

Article 16 makes clear that after notification of a wrongful removal or retention, a judicial or administrative authority must not decide on the merits of rights of custody until the Hague return request has been finalised. Where a Central Authority or its intermediary is aware that a request for return has been received, and a custody petition has been filed, they should remind the court of its obligations under Article 16.

4.9 Reasons for refusing to accept an application

The Central Authority may reject an application "when it is manifest that the requirements of the Convention are not fulfilled" or the application is not "well-founded". The requirements are set out in Chapter 4.5.

The Central Authority must inform the applicant or the requesting Central Authority of the reasons for refusing to accept an application for return, according to Article 27.

Rejection of an application is a regrettable step, but sometimes it is necessary. A person may nevertheless be entitled to apply direct to the courts of another country if their application to the Central Authority is rejected (*see* Article 29). However, Central Authorities must exercise extreme caution before rejecting an application, especially where there is a difference of opinion between Central Authorities concerning habitual residence or rights of custody, as these issues will require judicial determination.

It would assist the maintenance of good relations and reduce any hostility flowing from the rejection, if the requested Central Authority notified the requesting Central Authority informally at first of the likely intention to reject the application. The requesting Central Authority may then be able to revise or improve the application to avoid its rejection or otherwise discuss the application before a formal notification of rejection to the Central Authority is made.

4.10 Locate the child

To proceed with the application, it is necessary to confirm that the child is actually in the requested country. Article 7(a) of the Convention imposes an obligation on Central Authorities to take appropriate steps to help locate a child.

Unfortunately, it appears that some Central Authorities have refused to assist, or failed to assist, in locating a child. Some Central Authorities have also been criticised for not

---

[37] Australian Family Court Rules, Order 2, rule 7; Austria: decision of the Supreme Court of 27 April 1999.

acting quickly to locate a child. On the other hand, the requesting Central Authority also has an obligation to provide all relevant information concerning the child. The Central Authority will usually be reliant on the applicant to provide that information.

To facilitate locating the child, it would be desirable if locating agencies were linked to Central Authorities, either formally or informally.

As a minimum standard, Central Authorities should use their best endeavours to locate a child. It must be remembered that for some Central Authorities, working with police to locate a child can be difficult if parental child abduction is not a criminal offence.

Some countries have appointed a liaison officer in the police force to work with Central Authorities on child abduction cases.[38] *See also* Chapter 6.2 "Education and Training".

Central Authorities should explain in their brochure/flyer/website the extent of their network for locating children. If there is no network or assistance available, except for the police, it should be made clear to applicants whether there are any private locating services or organisations to search for the child, and if so, how can they be contacted.

Central Authorities attempting to locate children should be able to obtain information from other governmental agencies and authorities and to communicate such information to interested authorities. Where possible, their enquiries should be exempted from legislation or regulations concerning the confidentiality of such information.[39]

This does not necessarily mean that the information will be passed on to the applicant. Indeed, in most cases, the applicant in the requesting country does not need to know the location of the child for the purposes of the return proceedings. If there are particular reasons why the applicant should not be told the child's location, (for example, concern for the safety of the child) and the requesting authority cannot give a guarantee of confidentiality, then the requested Central Authority should not disclose the information to the requesting authority.

Interpol can play a constructive and helpful role in locating abducted children. It is not necessary to institute criminal proceedings in order to seek such help, which may be obtained on the basis of a missing persons report, and indeed criminal proceedings may be counter-productive in particular cases. Central Authorities of a number of countries systematically discourage the institution of such proceedings. It is up to each country to determine what use could be made of the Interpol communications network, in connection with child abductions.[40]

See Appendix 5.1 for a list of measures taken by Central Authorities to help locate children.

4.11 Child not located or moved to another territory

If it is known that a child is not in the requested country, the application and documents should be returned to the requesting Central Authority. If the child's location is not known, the requested Central Authority should co-operate with the requesting authority to keep the case open and keep looking for the child for a reasonable period of time.

---

[38] Canada, Switzerland, Israel.
[39] Conclusion 1.9, Fourth Special Commission.
[40] Conclusion 6, Second Special Commission.

If a child is no longer in the territory of the requested Contracting State, the Central Authority has an obligation under Article 9 to promptly transmit the application to another Central Authority where the child is thought to be.

This obligation to transmit the application promptly becomes important if the 12 month time limit for a mandatory return is approaching (*see* Article 12(1)), or if the first requested Central Authority has all the original documentation which will be needed by the second requested Central Authority.

4.12 Voluntary return

Child abduction cases, like domestic custody cases, should if possible be settled by consent between the parties. The outcomes are better for all concerned if this can be achieved, bearing in mind that, like custody disputes, not every case is suited to a consensual settlement.

Article 7(c) of the Convention imposes an obligation on Central Authorities to take all appropriate measures to obtain the voluntary return of the child or to resolve matters amicably. This obligation is emphasised by its repetition in Article 10. It is the role of the Central Authority to take appropriate steps to initiate a voluntary return, in accordance with Article 7(c). Many Central Authorities may themselves be actively involved in voluntary return negotiations. The Central Authority is not obligated to negotiate a voluntary return, but in appropriate cases it should provide information to the applicant and the abductor, and their legal representatives, concerning the obligations of Article 7(c) and Article 10, and the advantages of a voluntary return.

See sample letter at Appendix 4.2.

In countries with a high return rate, abductors often choose to return a child voluntarily when they are informed about the operation of the Convention, and are made aware that they face expensive legal proceedings, and that their prospects of success are usually low.

The advantages of a voluntary return were set out in Working Document No 9 at the Fourth Special Commission. Voluntary returns are advantageous because:

- the disruption to the child is minimal;

- the polarisation of parties' attitudes resulting from court action is avoided;

- the chance of a satisfactory long term solution is greater;

- hostility between the parties over future access arrangements may be avoided.

Other benefits of a voluntary return include:

- potentially less trauma for the child;

- a level of agreement between the parents can reduce tensions upon return;

- legal expenses and time in court are reduced;

- parents can agree to certain conditions to facilitate the return.

Central Authorities should as a matter of practice seek to achieve voluntary return, as intended by Article 7(c) of the Convention, where possible and appropriate by instructing to this end legal agents involved, whether state lawyers or private practitioners, or by referral of parties to a specialist organisation providing an appropriate mediation service. The role played by the courts in this regard is also recognised.[41]

In some cases, it is necessary to seek a balance between ensuring speed and achieving an amicable resolution, if this approach will best serve the child's interests. If extra time is spent and an amicable resolution is reached, this is still a good outcome. But Central Authorities or their intermediaries should act quickly to terminate negotiations about an amicable resolution or voluntary return if it becomes apparent that this is simply a delaying tactic by the abductor.[42]

Measures employed to assist in securing the voluntary return of the child or to bring about an amicable resolution of the issues should not result in any undue delay in return proceedings.[43]

In some countries, when a parent has sought return of the child so that regular access or contact could be enjoyed in the habitual residence country, negotiations have resulted in that parent agreeing to the child remaining with the custodial parent provided the access rights were respected.

To secure the voluntary return of the child or bring about an amicable settlement (including mediation), some Central Authorities take particular steps prior to filing a return petition. These steps include:

- sending a letter to the respondent parent requesting a voluntary return;

- making direct contact with the respondent parent;

- considering the risk of flight;

- obtaining orders from the competent court (e.g. non-removal order);

- providing referral to mediation services;

- providing referral to counselling and social services;

- relying on counsel, parent or outside agencies to negotiate;

- sending the letter of request for return simultaneously with the filing of the return petition, to avoid delay and encourage a voluntary return.

Negotiations for a voluntary return are unlikely to be successful when:

- there is a risk of further flight;

- the hostile behaviour of either or both parents is an indicator of likely failure;

- there is or has been a history of violence between the parties.

---

[41] Conclusion 1.10, Fourth Special Commission.
[42] *See* Article 7 and Conclusions 1.10-1.12, Fourth Special Commission.
[43] Conclusion 1.11, Fourth Special Commission.

4.13 Arrange or assist with legal representation for the applicant

Central Authorities have an obligation under Article 7(g), where the circumstances so require, to take all appropriate measures to provide or facilitate the provision of legal aid or advice, including the participation of legal counsel and advisers.

The First Special Commission saw a correlation between the obligations of Central Authorities under Article 7(f) to assist in the initiation of court proceedings for return of a child and the reservation under Article 26 concerning lawyers' fees, made by a number of States. Countries with broad territories and either no legal aid system or territorially non-unified legal aid had experienced or might experience in the future difficulties in obtaining legal representation for applicants who could not afford legal fees. The Special Commission encourages such States to intensify their efforts to obtain legal counsel or advisers in order to avoid serious prejudice to the interests of the children involved.[44]

The role of the Central Authorities in providing or facilitating the provision of legal aid and advice varies considerably. Various practices of Central Authorities include:

- information provided on methods of obtaining legal aid and advice, and options for assistance;

- applications for legal aid are facilitated;

- referral to reduced fee or *pro bono* lawyer(s);

- representation by the Central Authorities or State Attorneys;

- return proceedings are free of cost;

- legal costs are met by Central Authorities or Legal Aid Offices.

In so far as their powers or functions permit, Central Authorities should be alert to the problems caused by the following obstacles to the Convention:

- delays resulting from the required payment of retainers for legal representatives in the requested State;

- delays caused by means/merits tests for legal aid.

4.14 Provide follow-up information promptly

Simple procedures should be developed to provide follow-up information about applications. Some information about the immediate steps being taken should be provided, preferably with the acknowledgement of receipt. Central Authorities must recognise the anxiety of the left behind parent to know what is happening with the application.

Prompt replies to communications will save time and effort for all parties, even if the reply is to advise on a lack of progress. Prompt replies also build confidence that the application is being monitored carefully.

---

[44] Conclusion VI, First Special Commission.

A procedure to inform the requesting Central Authority promptly (if developments are occurring rapidly) or regularly (if progress is slow) will discourage excessive requests for progress reports from the requesting Central Authority which is under endless pressure from the left behind parent.

Email is the quickest method to provide follow-up information or progress reports. If resources are limited and email is not available, a standard form or letter can be used to provide progress reports. For example, the standard form or letter can advise if:

- the application has been referred to a lawyer or court for action;

- the police or other agencies are searching for the child;

- a date has been set for a court hearing.

There is a further obligation on Central Authorities or their intermediaries in Article 7(d) to exchange information about the child's social background, where it is desirable to do so. Sometimes, as part of the administrative procedures or the legal proceedings for the return of a child, lawyers, judges or administrators require additional information about the social situation that an abducted child has left behind, or to which the child will return.

The court or Central Authority which requests this information should be reasonable in the nature and extent of its demands. The Central Authority which is asked to provide this information should be tolerant of the requirements of courts and tribunals in the other country, especially if it will facilitate the return of the child. It is also important to note that in the common law system, if a Central Authority or a lawyer representing an applicant fails to provide information requested by the court, the Central Authority or lawyer may be in contempt of court orders. In civil law countries, the application may not be pursued by the court seized, if information is requested and not provided.

4.15 Take steps to prevent further harm to the child or prejudice to interested parties

Article 7(b) requires Central Authorities or their intermediaries to take all appropriate measures to prevent further harm to a child or prejudice to interested parties by taking or causing to be taken provisional measures.

The Central Authority, its intermediary or other agencies will sometimes become aware that a child's life or welfare is at risk in the country of refuge. It is recognised that the ability of Central Authorities to act in such circumstances depends on the limits of the powers vested in them. The Central Authority should, at the very least, be able to alert other welfare or child protection agencies when a child is at risk, so that those agencies can take necessary protective measures. Some Central Authorities have been given power to apply direct to a court for protection orders.[45]

It is important for a requesting Central Authority to provide full information about its concerns for a child's safety to enable protective measures to be instituted in the requested country.

---

[45] Quebec: An Act Respecting the Civil Aspects of International and Interprovincial Child Abduction, 1985. R.S.Q., c. A-23.01, section 11; Australia: Family Law (Child Abduction Convention) Regulations, regulation 14(1)(d);

Contracting States should ensure the availability of effective procedures to prevent either party from removing the child prior to the decision on return.[46]

Further harm to the child could arise from:

- the risk of re-abduction and concealment – by the abductor or by the other parent;

- remaining in the care of an abusive or threatening abductor;

- being refused contact with the other parent or family members;

Prejudice to interested parties may arise if:

- the abductor prolongs the proceedings, and the child becomes settled, and there is a risk of psychological harm to the child if he/she is forced to return to the habitual residence country after a long absence;

- the abductor deliberately alienates the child from the absent parent;

- the left behind parent is unable to get legal representation.

4.16 Initiate or facilitate legal proceedings

Article 7(f) imposes an obligation on Central Authorities to initiate or facilitate the institution of legal or administrative proceedings to obtain the return of the child.

Central Authorities are not themselves required to initiate legal proceedings. However, they should monitor the progress of applications to ensure that legal or other proceedings for return are commenced by the appropriate person or agency.

Most Central Authorities do not participate in any stage of the legal proceedings, although they may instruct or advise the applicant's legal representative. In some States the Central Authority is the applicant in the proceedings, or represents the applicant parent directly or is present as *amicus curiae.*

Representation of a parent directly by a Central Authority may cause problems if the other parent later becomes an applicant.

Legal proceedings may be commenced even if a voluntary return is contemplated. In common law countries, consent orders for return may be obtained without the need for a defended hearing. (Consent orders are orders made with the consent or agreement of both parties.) In civil law countries, an agreement of the parties may be incorporated into a court settlement. In this sense, it is equivalent to consent orders, as without incorporation, the agreement has no legal effect. An order having legal effect, either by consent or agreement, may be helpful if, at some point in the future, enforcement of the order becomes necessary.

---

[46] Conclusion 1.12, Fourth Special Commission.

4.17 Minimise requirements for applicants to attend court hearings in the requested country

If a child is taken to a distant country, the foreign applicant is faced with problems not encountered by an applicant whose child is taken to a neighbouring country. In these circumstances the distant foreign applicant may face:

- a heavy financial burden from expensive travel and accommodation costs in the requested country;

- an additional financial burden when time off work is taken;

- possible penalties or loss of job if too much time is taken;

- time constraints if travelling long distances at short notice to attend the hearing.

Where a court has a discretion to require the applicant's attendance at the hearing of the return proceedings, the Central Authority may try, through the applicant's legal representative, to inform the court of the difficulties faced by a foreign applicant in these circumstances. The use of telephone or videoconferencing facilities may provide a satisfactory solution. For a discussion of this issue as an implementing measure, *see* Chapter 6.5.3 of Guide to Good Practice, Part II - Implementing Measures.

4.18 Monitor progress of the application

Monitoring of progress of the application should be done in accordance with the established timeframes or timescales in the office procedures manual (*see* 4.1 above).

The requested Central Authority should keep the requesting authority informed as to the progress or status of the case. This is particularly relevant where the information is of practical importance to the applicant, for example, where travel arrangements have to be made.

After the appointment of a legal representative for the applicant (irrespective of whether the appointment is by the court, the Central Authority or other method), the Central Authority must continue to monitor progress of the application. In some countries, the applicant's lawyer must report regularly to the Central Authority on progress and developments in the case.

Where the return request is handled by a private lawyer, the Central Authority should, if possible, be informed that the requirements for expedition are met.

Although the lawyer and the applicant may be in direct communication, and the Central Authority is not directly involved in the legal proceedings, ultimately it is the Central Authorities in each country which must explain and justify the operation of the Convention in their respective countries.

This monitoring is particularly important if the application is not proceeding in accordance with Convention standards and requirements. The Central Authority should take whatever measures are possible, within the scope of its powers and functions, to ensure that the legal representatives for the applicant and the respondent, as well as the judicial or administrative authority, are fully aware of their Convention obligations.

Of course, the final decision on the application rests with the judicial or administrative authority.

4.19 Inform requesting Central Authority as soon as a court decision is known

The applicant or requesting Central Authority should be informed as soon as a court decision is known. The decision will impact on:

- a possible appeal;

- arrangements for return;

- a risk of flight or re-abduction if the child is ordered to return.

The applicant should not be disadvantaged in any of these matters by a lack of prompt communication from the requested Central Authority or the applicant's lawyer.

4.20 Appeals

Take any appropriate steps to ensure that the requesting Central Authority or the applicant is aware of his/her rights of appeal, as well as any deadlines or conditions attached to the appeal. If the Central Authority has different administrative procedures to follow for appeals (compared to requests for return), for example, applying for further legal aid, these must be made known to the requesting Central Authority or applicant.

If the respondent appeals against a return order, ensure that the requesting Central Authority or the applicant is informed, and has an opportunity to submit additional material or evidence, if it is admissible. The applicant's lawyer should keep the requested Central Authority informed of the status of the appeal.

Information about the appeals process in the requested country should be available to interested parties well <u>before</u> an order for non-return is made, to avoid any disadvantage to the applicant. This type of information should be on the Central Authority's website, or in its brochure or flyer.

4.21 Practical arrangements for return of the child

Practical arrangements for the safe return of children should be under contemplation from the commencement of the application.[47] Co-operation between both the requested and requesting Central Authorities is needed to achieve the safe return of the child.

To this end, questions to consider here include:

- are there any particular safety or security issues;

- who will accompany the child home;

- who will pay for the child's travel expenses;

---

[47] Conclusion 4, Second Special Commission.

- does the applicant have to initiate separate legal proceedings to enforce the return order;

- if so, is the applicant aware of this.

Central Authorities or the appropriate agencies should act quickly to prevent re-abduction of a child following a return order, or at any other stage of the proceedings.

4.22 Conditions or undertakings attached to the return order should be reasonable

Conditions or undertakings attached to a return order are employed in certain legal systems to facilitate return of children; for example, to make temporary arrangements for the necessities of life such as accommodation, food, financial support; to provide for the safety and welfare of the child. Central Authorities should be aware of the current practices relating to conditions and undertakings in their countries and should make the information available to other Central Authorities.

There has been much discussion in international meetings on this subject, and in common law countries, there is some agreement that undertakings may be used if limited in scope and duration, and done in furtherance of the Convention's goal of ensuring the prompt return of children to their habitual residence.[48] While various views have been put forward regarding the proper scope of such undertakings or conditions, there appears to be general agreement among many common law countries on the issue of duration: namely that undertakings or conditions should be interim in nature, having effect only up to the time that the court of the habitual residence is seized of the relevant issues.

See also Chapters 3.20 and 3.21.

4.23 Issues or concerns about safe return

If a return is to be ordered, the Central Authority may be consulted on any issues or concerns about the safe return of the child or parent. If such issues exist, the requested and requesting Central Authorities should co-operate with each other to achieve a safe return. If there are communications between judges in the requested and requesting countries to achieve a safe return, the Central Authorities may be involved in facilitating them.

Article 7(h) requires Central Authorities to take all appropriate measures to provide necessary administrative arrangements to secure the safe return of the child. The role of the Central Authorities (requested and requesting) in securing the safe return of the child was discussed in considerable detail at previous Special Commissions, in particular, the Special Commissions of 1997 and 2001.

---

[48] *Re C ((A Minor) Abduction)* [1989] 1 FLR 403 [INCADAT cite: HC/E/UKe 34]; *Re O (Child Abduction: Undertakings)* [1994] 2 FLR 349 [INCADAT cite: HC/E/UKe 85]; *Re M (Abduction: Undertakings)* [1995] 1 FLR 1021 [INCADAT cite: HC/E/UKe 20]. For a comprehensive review of the issue of undertakings generally, see *Issues Surrounding the Safe Return of the Child (and the Custodial Parent)*, a paper presented by the Australian Delegation at International Child Custody: A Common Law Judicial Conference, 18-21 September 2000 in Washington, DC.

See Chapter 3.18 for a discussion of the issues and practices around safe return. These issues and practices may apply equally to the requested or the requesting State in an individual case.

It is recognised that the protection of the child may also sometimes require steps to be taken to protect an accompanying parent.

4.24 Information for returning parents

If a return is to be ordered, the requested and requesting Central Authorities should co-operate to ensure that the abductor who wishes to return with the child is informed about services or assistance available in the requesting country. This is so even if there are no concerns or issues about a safe return, as discussed above and at Chapters 3.18, 3.20 and 6.3.

4.25 Assistance with enforcement of a return order

Effective enforcement is a key to the successful operation of the Convention.

Assistance with enforcement of a return order may be sought from police or other agencies. In some countries which are heavily dependent on air travel (*e.g.* Hong Kong, South Africa, New Zealand, Australia), the Central Authority may request police assistance to ensure a child is put on his/her approved flight. This type of assistance may not be feasible in Europe, USA or Canada if return is by train or car.

4.26 Confirmation of return

A Central Authority should seek confirmation from the requesting Central Authority that the child (and parent) has (have) returned. If conditions were attached to the return, a request should be made for confirmation that these conditions were met (usually by the applicant and sometimes by the abductor).

Although there is no specific obligation imposed by the Convention to confirm the return of a child, it is in the interests of Contracting States and their Central Authorities to do so, insofar as is possible. Without such information, it is impossible for Contracting States and their Central Authorities to know whether the fundamental objectives of the Convention have been met.

It is recognised that the protection of the child may also sometimes require steps to be taken to protect an accompanying parent.

4.27 Maximise opportunities to inform the professions about the principles and procedures of the Hague Convention

Within the limits of the implementing arrangements in each country, Central Authorities should use any opportunities arising from the handling of applications to inform legal and other professionals, including courts and judges, about the principles and procedures of the 1980 Hague Convention.

5.   SUMMARY: ACCESS APPLICATIONS: ROLE OF REQUESTING AND REQUESTED CENTRAL AUTHORITIES

Preliminary observations

- Article 21 facilitates access arrangements and requires Central Authorities to remove, as far as possible, all obstacles to the exercise of such rights

- Article 7(f) imposes an obligation to take all appropriate measures to make arrangements in a proper case for organising or securing the effective exercise of rights of access

- Articles 7 and 21 together require Central Authorities to co-operate in promoting the peaceful enjoyment of access rights

- specific measures that Central Authorities can take depend on the nature and extent of their powers to act

- deficiencies in the Convention in securing protection for rights of access have been recognised

A.   OUTLINE OF PROCEDURE FOR THE REQUESTING CENTRAL AUTHORITY (OUTGOING APPLICATIONS)

Preparing and sending applications

5.1   Obtain information about procedures in the requested country

5.2   Check that the application is complete and in an acceptable form for the requested country

5.3   Check that the application satisfies Convention requirements

5.4   Provide information about relevant laws

5.5   Ensure all essential supporting documents are included

5.6   Provide a translation of the application and all essential documents

5.7   Ensure the application is sent to the correct mailing address, fax number or email address of the requested Central Authority

5.8   Send the original application by priority mail, and fax or email an advance copy of the application

5.9   If the application is very urgent, highlight the reasons for the urgency

Assisting and responding to the requested Central Authority

5.10   If the requested Central Authority requires additional information, ensure that all the information is provided promptly

5.11   Advise the requested Central Authority if there are difficulties in meeting their deadlines

5.12   Be reasonable about requests for follow-up information

5.13   Monitor progress of the application

Assisting with the effective exercise of access rights

5.14   Assistance available in the requesting country

5.15   Assistance if access is to take place in the requesting country

5.16   Co-operate with the requested Central Authority to ensure agreed arrangements are observed

B.   OUTLINE OF PROCEDURE FOR THE REQUESTED CENTRAL AUTHORITY (INCOMING APPLICATIONS)

Receiving and acknowledging applications

5.17   Establishing timeframes for dealing with applications

5.18   Applications may be received by mail, fax or email

5.19   Register the receipt of the application on an internal register

5.20   Acknowledge receipt of the application

5.21   Check the application to ensure Convention requirements are satisfied

5.22   If additional information or documents are required, advise the requesting Central Authority in the acknowledgement letter/email or in a follow-up letter/email

5.23   If the Central Authority decides not to accept the application, inform the requesting Central Authority of the reasons

Actions following acceptance of the application

5.24   Locate the child and confirm that he/she is actually in the requested country

5.25   If the child is not located, return the application

5.26   If the application meets the Convention requirements, consider if voluntary contact arrangements are appropriate and feasible

5.27   Arrange legal representation for the applicant or assist the applicant to obtain legal representation

Assisting with the effective exercise of access rights

5.28   Provide the requesting Central Authority with follow-up information about action taken on behalf of the applicant

5.29   Ensure that the procedures permitted by the administrative and judicial system of the requested country are followed

5.30   Take steps to prevent further harm to the child or prejudice to interested parties, if feasible and appropriate

5.31   Attendance of applicants at court hearings in the requested country will depend on the individual circumstances of the case

5.32   Monitor progress of the application

5.33   Assist with implementing or enforcing access orders

5. ACCESS APPLICATIONS: ROLE OF REQUESTING AND REQUESTED CENTRAL AUTHORITIES

PRELIMINARY OBSERVATIONS

The Fourth Meeting of the Special Commission to review the operation of the *Hague Convention of 25 October 1980 on the Civil Aspects of International Child Abduction* held on 22-28 March 2001 recognised the deficiencies of the Convention in achieving the objective of securing protection for rights of access in transfrontier situations, and regarded it as a serious problem requiring urgent attention in the interests of the children and parents concerned.[49]

Article 21 provides for application to be made to a Central Authority "to make arrangements for organising or securing the effective exercise of rights of access". The Central Authorities are bound by the Article 7 obligations of co-operation "to promote the peaceful enjoyment of access rights and the fulfilment of any conditions to which the exercise of those rights may be subject". They are bound to take steps "to remove, as far as possible, all obstacles to the exercise of such rights", and they may directly or indirectly initiate or assist in the institution of proceedings in a proper case "with a view to organising or protecting those rights and securing respect for the conditions to which the exercise of those rights may be subject".

As the Pérez-Vera Report points out,[50] the precise ways in which the Central Authorities are required to co-operate under Article 21 (with the exception of removing obstacles as far as possible), in securing the exercise of access rights is "left up to the co-operation among the Central Authorities", and the specific measures which Central Authorities are able to take "will depend on the circumstances of each case and on the capacity to act enjoyed by each Central Authority".

There are also differences of practice with regard to the jurisdictional implications of Article 21. Does it apply only in the abduction context, for example, where a return application is pending or has been refused, or does it apply generally? Does it apply only where rights of access have already been established by court order, or can it be used to establish such rights?

In the absence of certainty or agreement on the interpretation of Article 21, this chapter must be confined to areas of common understanding. Emphasis is on the importance of co-operation within the agreed scope of the Convention.

Note: The problems and issues surrounding the access provisions have been discussed in the Final Report on Transfrontier Access/Contact and the *Hague Convention of 25 October 1980 on the Civil Aspects of International Child Abduction*, drawn up by William Duncan, Deputy Secretary General, for the attention of the Special Commission of September/October 2002.

Following discussion of this report the Special Commission made certain recommendations,[51] including continuation by the Permanent Bureau of work on a separate chapter of the Guide to Good Practice relating to transfrontier access/contact in the context of the 1980 Convention with the objectives of promoting consistent and best practices in relation to those matters which it is agreed fall within the competence

---

[49] Conclusion 6.1, Fourth Special Commission.
[50] *See* paragraph 127.
[51] *See* Conclusion 2, Special Commission concerning Special Commission concerning the *Hague Convention of 25 October 1980 on the Civil Aspects of International Child Abduction* held from 27 September to 1 October 2002.

and obligations of States Parties under the Convention, and providing examples of practice even in relation to matters which fall within the disputed areas of interpretation. It was also recommended that work should begin on the formulation of general principles and considerations which need to be borne in mind by Contracting States and their authorities when formulating policies in respect of international access / contact cases.

It is expected therefore that a separate chapter of the Guide to Good Practice will be published in due course devoted to the subject of transfrontier access applications in the context of the 1980 Convention.

A.   ROLE OF REQUESTING CENTRAL AUTHORITY

5.1   Obtain information about procedures in the requested country

The guidelines at Chapter 3.1 are relevant for step 5.1.

5.2   Check that the application is complete and in an acceptable form for the requested country

The guidelines at Chapter 3.2 are relevant here. It is important to be aware of the procedures for access applications in the requested country to ensure that the application fulfils any specific legal or administrative requirements of the requested country.

If it is known that a separate application for legal aid is required for Convention access cases, send the legal aid application with the access application to save time. Copies of the necessary legal aid form should be provided by the requested Central Authority, with guidance on how to complete the form, where it is unclear to a foreign applicant.

5.3   Check that the application satisfies Convention requirements

This is explained in Chapter 5.21.

The guidelines in Chapters 3.5 to 3.9 are relevant for steps 5.4 to 5.8.

5.4   Provide information about relevant laws

5.5   Ensure all essential supporting documents are included

See Checklist at Appendix 3.7.

5.6   Provide a translation of the application and all essential documents

5.7   Ensure the application is sent to the correct address or fax or email number of the requested Central Authority

5.8   Send the original application by priority mail, and fax or email an advance copy of the application

5.9 Urgent applications

It is generally agreed that access applications do not have the same degree of urgency as requests for return. This does not make access applications any less important, given their role as a preventive measure for abductions.

Access applications may become urgent in situations where:

- a child is supposed to travel abroad alone for an access visit and the custodial parent refuses, or will refuse to honour the arrangements;

- the access parent has travelled or intends to travel to visit the child and the custodial parent has indicated the child will not be available for the visit;

- a child has been located after a long period of searching, and the access parent is anxious to re-establish contact.

The guidelines in Chapters 3.11 to 3.13 are relevant for steps 5.10 to 5.12.

5.10 If the requested Central Authority requires additional information, ensure that all the information is provided promptly

5.11 Advise the requested Central Authority if there are difficulties in meeting their deadlines

5.12 Be reasonable about requests for follow-up information

5.13 Monitor progress of the application

See Chapters 3.14 and 4.18 for a discussion of the requested and requesting Central Authorities' monitoring responsibilities. If there is no progress because of the intransigence of the custodial parent, discuss enforcement options with the requested authority.

5.14 Assistance available in the requesting country

Some of the measures of "Assistance with implementing or enforcing access orders" discussed in Chapter 5.33 apply equally to requesting and requested Central Authorities.

5.15 Assistance if access is to take place in the requesting country

If the child is to travel to the requesting country for an access visit, there are a number of steps the requesting authority can take, including:

- advising the custodial parent to obtain a written programme or itinerary for the access visit, with names, addresses and telephone numbers of people and places to be visited. If the child is not returned, and the parent and child go into hiding, the programme details may assist to locate the child;

- obtaining a copy of this programme or itinerary;

- ensuring that the parent and child have the telephone numbers of support services, should any problems arise during the visit.

5.16 Co-operate with the requested Central Authority to ensure agreed arrangements are observed

Where conditions or safeguards have been attached to the exercise of access or contact, take whatever steps are possible to ensure that the conditions are observed.

It is necessary to ensure that the access parent understands that a failure to observe any agreed conditions may result in the court or custodial parent refusing future visits.

B.   ROLE OF REQUESTED CENTRAL AUTHORITY

Article 21 makes clear that an access application may be presented to a requested Central Authority in the same way as a request for return. It is apparent from the outline of procedures in the Summary at the beginning of this chapter that administratively, there is little difference in handling incoming abduction and access applications up to the point of accepting the application.

Steps 5.17 to 5.20 are similar to the abduction procedures in Chapter 4.1 to 4.4. Those steps have been described in detail in Chapter 4, and that information need not be repeated.

5.17 Establish timeframes for dealing with applications

5.18 Applications may be received by mail, fax or email

5.19 Register the receipt of the application on an internal register

5.20 Acknowledge receipt of the application

5.21 Ensure Convention requirements are satisfied

The good practice guidelines for checking and processing of return applications apply equally to access applications. The basic, commonly agreed requirements to be satisfied are:

- the child is habitually resident in a Convention country; and

- the child is not yet 16 years of age.

Sample checklists are at Appendices 3.7 and 3.8. However, any checklist must reflect the different requirements and approaches taken in Contracting States.

After acceptance of the application and reporting on the next procedural or legal steps to the requesting Central Authority, there is considerable divergence of practice between States in handling access applications.

Steps 5.22 to 5.26 below are similar to the abduction procedures in Chapter 4.6, 4.9 to 4.11. Those steps have been described in detail in Chapter 4, and that information need not be repeated here. A sample voluntary access letter is at Appendix 4.5.

5.22 If additional information or documents are required, advise the requesting Central Authority in the acknowledgement letter/email or in a follow-up letter/email

5.23 If the Central Authority decides not to accept the application, inform the requesting Central Authority of the reasons

5.24 Take steps to locate the child and confirm that he/she is actually in the requested country

5.25 If the child is not located, return the application

5.26 If the application meets the Convention requirements, consider if voluntary contact arrangements are appropriate and feasible

5.27 Access to legal aid and advice, or legal representation

Central Authorities should do everything possible to provide or facilitate legal aid and advice to the access parent.

The role of the Central Authorities in providing or facilitating the provision of legal aid and advice varies considerably. Many countries require the applicant to apply for legal aid, on the same terms and conditions as a resident or citizen of that country. Other Central Authorities treat access applications the same as return applications in terms of legal representation for the applicant: in other words, the applicant may have to bear all the legal costs, or none of them, depending on the country in question.

Various practices of Central Authorities regarding legal aid for access applications include:

- information provided on methods of obtaining legal aid and advice, and options for assistance;

- applications for legal aid are facilitated;

- referral to reduced fee or *pro bono* lawyer(s);

- representation by the Central Authorities or State lawyers;

- access proceedings are free of cost;

- legal costs met by Central Authorities or Legal Aid Offices.

5.28 Provide follow-up information

The comments at Chapter 4.14 are relevant for step 5.28.

5.29 Ensure that the procedures permitted by the administrative and judicial system of the requested country are followed

The guidelines at Chapter 4.15 and 4.17 are relevant for steps 5.30 and 5.31.

5.30 Take steps to prevent further harm to the child or prejudice to interested parties, if feasible and appropriate

5.31 Attendance of applicants at court hearings in the requested country will depend on the individual circumstances of the case

5.32 Monitor progress of the application

Access can be difficult to monitor according to any set timeframes. Like domestic access disputes, transfrontier disputes have particular difficulties:

- they may drag on for long periods;

- there may be little or no progress over that time;

- the custodial parent can easily undermine planned access arrangements (even court ordered arrangements);

- undermining arrangements or breaching court orders is especially problematic when the access parent from abroad is visiting the child's country and only has a limited time there;

- the custodial parent can exhaust the access parent's emotional, physical and financial resources by constant failure to observe agreed arrangements.

5.33 Assistance with implementing or enforcing access orders

The extent to which the requested Central Authority can assist with implementing or enforcing access orders will vary from country to country. Some of the measures of assistance offered by different Central Authorities include:

- support from social or youth/child welfare services, for example, where supervision of access is required;

- support from social or youth/child welfare services when measures are needed to accustom a child to contact after a long period of separation;

- contacting the International Social Service (ISS) for assistance;

- use of supervised visitation centres;

- arranging and funding supervised access in certain difficult cases;

- arranging and funding telephone access;

- acting as a post box for letters where the child's address cannot be disclosed.

6. SUMMARY: OTHER IMPORTANT FUNCTIONS AND ISSUES FOR CENTRAL AUTHORITIES

6.1 The maintenance of statistics

- Central Authorities should maintain accurate Convention statistics

- Central Authorities should make annual returns of statistics to the Permanent Bureau

- A statistical database (INCASTAT) will be established as a complement to the International Child Abduction Database (INCADAT)

- Collecting and sending reliable statistics is an additional demand on the resources of Central Authorities. If necessary they should seek assistance to develop accurate statistical recording processes

6.2 Education and training

- The Convention generally works well in the interests of children and meets the needs for which it was drafted

- However, education of the general public and the legal and welfare professions about the Convention remains a priority, and Central Authorities should take an active role to achieve this goal

- Preventing child abduction through public education is important and Central Authorities should try to reach the widest audience through various methods of information dissemination

6.3 Issues surrounding the safe return of children and parents

- Concerning safe return orders, the issue is to obtain in the requesting jurisdiction any provisional protective measures prior to the return of the child

- Concerning criminal proceedings, the issue is to take into account the impact of a criminal prosecution for child abduction on the possibility of achieving a return of the child

- Concerning immigration matters, the issue is to take measures to ensure that generally the abducting parent will be permitted to re-enter the requesting country to participate in custody or access proceedings

- Concerning the provision of legal aid and advice, the issue is to take measures to ensure that parents have access to a country's legal system to adequately present their case in custody proceedings following a child's return

6.4   Repatriation

- Central Authorities should give consideration to practical forms of assistance for repatriating children to their habitual residence country

6.5   Twinning arrangements

- A "twinning" arrangement could arise if a developing Central Authority seeks assistance from an experienced Central Authority to provide advice, materials, training and possibly an exchange of personnel for practical training and experience

6.6   The 1996 Hague Convention on Child Protection

- The 1996 Convention has potential advantages as an adjunct to the 1980 Convention, and Contracting States are recommended to consider ratification or accession

6.7   Prevention

6.7.1   Information

6.7.2   Education

6.7.3   Co-operation

6.7.4   Legislation

6.8   Enforcement

The enforcement of return orders will be improved if the following matters are addressed in each Contracting State:

- Effective mechanisms for enforcement are included in implementing measures, including implementing legislation;

- Co-operation between the judicial authority and the enforcement agency;

- Clear directions in the return order about how the return arrangements are to be effected;

- Any necessary precautionary measures to reduce the risk of flight by the abductor with the child after the return order is made.

6. OTHER IMPORTANT FUNCTIONS AND ISSUES FOR CENTRAL AUTHORITIES

6.1 The maintenance of statistics

Central Authorities are encouraged to maintain accurate statistics concerning the cases dealt with by them under the Convention, and to make annual returns of statistics to the Permanent Bureau in accordance with the standard forms established by the Permanent Bureau in consultation with Central Authorities.[52]

The importance of accurate statistics from a large number of Contacting States has been highlighted by the valuable research and analysis done by Professor Nigel Lowe and his team at Cardiff University into all 1999 Hague cases.[53] The results have confirmed certain beliefs about the Convention and overturned others.

The Permanent Bureau's plan to establish a statistical database (INCASTAT) as a complement to the International Child Abduction Database (INCADAT) has been endorsed, and Contracting States have been encouraged to consider methods by which the resources for the project may be made available.[54]

The Permanent Bureau will ensure that it sets clear parameters for the collection of data, and keep the process as simple as possible. However, statistics must contain sufficient detail to make them meaningful and useful. Briefly, the statistical data must be:

- simple

- accessible

- non-identifying

- privacy protected.

The collection of statistical data for the Permanent Bureau has improved since the Cardiff research project was developed. The Permanent Bureau needs the collection of accurate statistics to continue so that the planned statistical database can be developed and future global trends in child abduction can be analysed against the 1999 "snapshot" of cases. The categories of statistics requested by the Permanent Bureau, with the approved forms, are at Appendix 6.

The resource limitations of Central Authorities are recognised, and it is acknowledged that collecting and sending reliable statistics is a further demand on those resources. The "twinning" arrangement between developing and established Central Authorities, discussed in Chapters 2.5.2 and 6.5 may be one means whereby assistance or advice can be made available to develop accurate statistical recording processes.

---

[52] Conclusion 1.14, Fourth Special Commission.
[53] Statistical Analysis of Applications made in 1999 under the 1980 Convention. Final Report November 2001. Available on the Hague Conference website at <http://www.hcch.net>.
[54] Conclusion 1.15, Fourth Special Commission.

6.2 Education and training

Successive Special Commissions have agreed that in general the Convention works well in the interests of children and meets the needs for which it was drafted. However, education of the general public and the legal and welfare professions about the Convention remains a priority, not only in new Convention countries, but in long established Contracting States as well. It has been recognised that considerable and ongoing efforts must be made in order to promote fuller understanding of the Convention on the part of judges, lawyers and administrative authorities, as well as parents and other persons exercising responsibility for children.[55]

Central Authorities are in a unique position to take an active role in informing the public and the legal and welfare professions about child abduction. This education role extends beyond training its own Central Authority personnel, and includes training the personnel in other organisations and bodies whose assistance may be or will be required in implementing the Convention. Where possible, Central Authorities should seek funding and develop partnerships for education and training programmes. Central Authorities should take an active role in identifying any weaknesses in securing the delivery of the objects of the Convention.[56]

Education programmes may be conducted through:

- lectures and presentations as part of regular training courses for lawyers, judges, social workers, police, consular officers, process servers or other professionals as appropriate;

- conferences, seminars and workshops on a local, regional or multi-jurisdictional basis;[57]

- presentations at conferences for professionals in related disciplines;

- inclusion of child abduction issues in law school curricula;

- visits to Central Authorities or exchange of personnel between jurisdictions.

In developing education and training programmes, Central Authorities should seek advice and assistance from a broad range of experts, such as:

- the Permanent Bureau, which has developed, conducted and participated in national and regional training seminars and international judicial seminars;

- intergovernmental agencies and bodies, *e.g.* Commonwealth Secretariat;

- non-government organisations, *e.g.* Reunite, National Center for Missing and Exploited Children;

---

[55] Conclusion II, First Special Commission.
[56] In Switzerland, the Central Authority is active in informing other government departments about the Convention, the responsibilities of the government generally and the role of the Central Authority in particular; it organises seminars with relevant professionals; it encourages university students to use its resources to do research on the Convention, and is active in fostering good relations with the media and the press. In Hungary, the Central Authority has created a network of specialist abduction lawyers who will assist and advise parents in country areas about the conduct of Hague access cases.
[57] Switzerland has a very efficient network of Cantonal co-ordinators and cantonal education programmes.

- foreign aid agencies or organisations, *e.g.* UNICEF, International Social Services.

Some Central Authorities have developed guidelines with their local police force to provide assistance in abduction cases.[58] In another country, a Ministerial Directive establishes and clarifies the relationship between the police and the Central Authority.[59] The Central Authority should nurture and maintain a good relationship with the police (and other agencies), especially if there is a lack of enthusiasm for or knowledge about abduction cases. The re-assignment to other duties of experienced police officers can mean that the Central Authority should be alert to maintaining the relationship with the new officers and keeping them informed of Convention matters.

The police may need special training in situations such as:

- taking a child into protective care; or

- where there is a danger to a child or parent when a child is taken into care.[60]

Educating the public about the subject of child abduction may have a preventative effect. Informing them of the assistance available through Central Authorities will facilitate a quicker reaction if a child abduction occurs. Reaching the wider audience of the general public may be achieved by the Central Authority through:

- preparing a brochure or pamphlet for display and distribution in social welfare centres, unemployment bureaux, legal aid offices, courts, child care centres, schools and public libraries;

- developing a website (*see* Chapter 1.3.4);

- publicising annual statistics with a Press Release;

- developing links with non-government organisations that can publicise the role of the Central Authority in the media (newspaper, magazines, radio, television);

- developing a [24 hour] help line and utilising free advertising for the number on milk cartons, business envelopes *e.g.* Telecom accounts or credit cards.

Resources should also be provided (at the time of establishing the Central Authority, and later) to publicise within its own territory the existence of the Central Authority and its functions. It is important to ensure that, within one's own country, government and non-government organisations are aware of the existence and functions of the Central Authority and have its contact details in order to refer potential clients.

It is important to ensure that any brochures, printed materials and websites are kept up-to-date.

Regular regional meetings between countries that share many abduction cases may allow them to discuss issues such as patterns of abduction, prevention strategies, immigration matters. Meetings with law and policy makers may allow opportunities to

---

[58] United Kingdom, Israel.
[59] Belgium.
[60] Switzerland uses an aide-memoire or memorandum of understanding to reinforce its education and training links with police and child protection agencies.

discuss the effective working of the national implementing legislation and the need for possible amendments.

6.3 Issues surrounding the safe return of children and parents

Experience has shown that some courts may be reluctant to order the return of abducted children unless the judges are satisfied that the child (and in some cases the abducting parent) can return safely to the requesting country. Some judges may wish to be satisfied that the basic needs of food, housing, financial support and access to justice can be provided in the requesting country.

The Fourth Special Commission considered at length the issues surrounding the safe and prompt return of the child (and the custodial parent, where relevant). A number of recommendations were made for Contracting States (rather than for Central Authorities) and they are listed here because of their importance for the success of the Convention generally, and because Central Authorities may be involved to some extent in their implementation.

Safe return orders

Contracting States should consider the provision of procedures for obtaining, in the jurisdiction to which the child is to be returned, any necessary provisional protective measures prior to the return of the child.[61]

Criminal proceedings

The courts in some Contracting States have been reluctant to order return of a child if the abducting parent will face criminal prosecution upon return. In certain cases, some courts may consider a return to be contrary to the best interests of the child if he/she is separated from the primary carer/abductor because of the criminal proceedings; or if the primary carer/abductor is prejudiced in any custody proceedings because of the criminal proceedings or a warrant of arrest.

The impact of a criminal prosecution for child abduction on the possibility of achieving a return of the child is a matter which should be capable of being taken into account in the exercise of any discretion which the prosecuting authorities have to initiate, suspend or withdraw charges.[62]

Immigration matters

In the past few years, there have been a number of cases where either:

(a)   a child was not returned (due to the risk of psychological harm) because the abducting parent's immigration status in the requesting country prevented their re-entry; or

(b)   a child was returned even though the abducting parent was unable to re-enter the requesting country for immigration reasons. Consequently the abducting parent could not personally participate in later custody proceedings, with possible adverse consequences for the best interests of the child.

Contracting States should, as far as possible, take measures to ensure that, save in exceptional cases, the abducting parent will be permitted to enter the country to which

---

[61] Conclusion 5.1, Fourth Special Commission.
[62] Conclusion 5.2, Fourth Special Commission.

the child is returned for the purpose of taking part in legal proceedings concerning custody or protection of the child.[63]

The provision of legal aid and advice

It is considered that a child's interests are best served if both parents can actively participate in custody proceedings following the return of the child under the Convention.

Contracting States should take measures to ensure that parents who participate in custody proceedings after a child's return are given adequate access to a country's legal system to adequately present their case.[64]

6.4 Repatriation

As part of its implementing measures, a Contracting State and its Central Authority should give consideration to the method of repatriating a child whose return has been ordered. In some cases a return order is made by a court but it cannot be enforced because neither parent has the funds to pay for the child's return, and the requested country has no programme to repatriate abducted children. This is a particular problem when a child has been abducted to a distant country.

In certain countries, the travel costs for the return of the child may be paid by:

- the government of the requested country;[65]

- the government of the requesting country;[66]

- a charitable organisation in the requesting country;

- special agreement between the Central Authority and the national airline of the requesting country.[67]

6.5 Twinning arrangements

Central Authorities should be creative in considering ways to improve education and training opportunities between them. A "twinning" arrangement could occur if a developing Central Authority sought assistance from an experienced Central Authority. Funds could be sought from the foreign aid budget.

The experienced Central Authority may then provide advice, materials, training and possibly an exchange of personnel for practical training and experience. The arrangement could extend to (or be confined to):

- helping to develop a website, brochure or flyer;

- helping to develop an office procedures manual;

---

[63] Conclusion 5.3, Fourth Special Commission.
[64] Conclusion 5.4, Fourth Special Commission.
[65] *For example*, Scotland, New Zealand.
[66] *For example*, Australia.
[67] This arrangement is available to repatriate children to Canada.

- donating equipment *e.g.* fax machine, computer, printer, paper;

- foster visits or exchanges of administrative and judicial officers.

Twinning might work best between countries of a similar size, and with the same language and legal system. However, differences should not deter Central Authorities from attempting a "twinning" programme. Reports of any such experiments should be shared with other Central Authorities and the Permanent Bureau, for the benefit of all.

6.6 The 1996 Hague Convention on Child Protection

In Recommendation 7.1, the Fourth Special Commission Meeting stated:

The Special Commission recognises the potential advantages of the *Hague Convention of 19 October 1996 on Jurisdiction, Applicable Law, Recognition, Enforcement and Co-operation in respect of Parental Responsibility and Measures for the Protection of Children* as an adjunct to the 1980 Convention, and recommends that Contracting States should consider ratification or accession.

6.7 Prevention

Prevention of child abduction means:

- Deterring abductions through instruments like the 1980 Convention;

- Taking early precautions to avert or discourage any possibility of an abduction;

- Taking active measures to protect a child from a real possibility of abduction;

- Taking emergency measures to thwart an attempted abduction of a child from the jurisdiction.

Prevention of child abduction involves a number of actors working together at both the national and international levels. Central Authorities can play an important role in informing and educating, but preventive measures will not be effective without the co-operation and assistance of other agencies and bodies working in the field.[68] Preventive measures in legislation may be necessary to authorise the relevant agencies to take appropriate action.

6.7.1 Information

The purpose of an information campaign is to reach the largest possible audience with relatively brief information of a general nature, but advice on how to obtain further assistance or information is essential.

---

[68] This discussion is intended as a brief outline only. The Permanent Bureau will produce a report on preventive measures, in accordance with recommendations from the Special Commission concerning the *Hague Convention of 25 October 1980 on the Civil Aspects of International Child Abduction* (27 September to 1 October 2002), with a view to the future publication of a Guide to Good Practice.

Central Authorities can play an effective role in developing and disseminating information about the risks and problems of child abduction and how to address these issues. A list of publications that deal with prevention issues is at Appendix 7. Awareness of risks is a first step in being able to take essential precautions.[69] Some methods that a Central Authority can utilise to disseminate information are outlined in Chapter 6.2 "Education and Training".

Publicity concerning the Convention itself may have a deterrent effect on a would-be abductor, or it may alert a parent to take steps to prevent an abduction.

6.7.2 Education

The purpose of an education and training programme is to target a more specialised audience, such as experts or professionals in related fields. It is particularly important that the first point of contact for a parent seeking assistance to deal with an actual or potential child abduction is well informed about the steps to take. The first point of contact for help is often the local police, but it may also be a lawyer, social worker, or non-government organisation.

Some Central Authorities are proactive in finding opportunities to initiate or participate in education and training programmes for those people whose work directly or indirectly supports the implementation of the Convention in their country.

Suggestions for education and training programmes that Central Authorities could undertake are outlined in Chapter 6.2 "Education and Training".

6.7.3 Co-operation

Co-operation is essential between agencies, bodies, organisations and others if preventive measures are to be successful. An awareness of the need for speedy action or response at certain times by certain bodies or agencies is an important aspect of the co-operative approach to prevention. For example, if a court makes an order that a child must not leave the country, this order must be served promptly on police or customs officers, as well as on other individuals or agencies affected by the order, in order for it to be enforced. Another area for possible co-operation is between the passport issuing agencies of two countries concerning the issue of passports to their dual nationals.

Some Central Authorities have formalised their co-operative relationships with other agencies by developing a memorandum of understanding or guidelines, to clarify their respective roles and improve understanding of operational issues.[70]

6.7.4 Legislation

Preventive measures in legislation are steps taken by national governments or parliaments. These measures, having the force of law, give authority to courts, police or other agencies to take steps to prevent the abduction of a child.

---

[69] *See*, for example, the *Child Abduction Prevention Packs* developed by Reunite. These are available from the Reunite website at <http://www.reunite.org/prevention.html>.
[70] *See* Chapter 6.2 "Education and Training".

In some countries, Central Authorities will be in a position to advise their law and policy makers on the need to legislate for certain preventive measures. Examples of such measures that may be found in the legislation or procedures of some Contracting States include:

- punitive measures for unlawful removal of children;[71]

- prohibition on a child leaving the jurisdiction without the necessary permissions;[72]

- powers to locate and detain a child;[73]

- powers to refuse the issue of passports to children without the necessary permissions;[74]

- discretion to judicial authorities to make appropriate preventive orders.[75]

6.8   Enforcement

The real success of the Convention as a remedy for child abduction can be measured, not by the number of return orders made, but by the number of return orders enforced. Unfortunately there is some discrepancy between the two.

The enforcement of return orders will be improved if the following matters are addressed in each Contracting State:

- effective mechanisms for enforcement are included in implementing measures, including implementing legislation;

- co-operation between the judicial authority and the enforcement agency;

- clear directions in the return order about how the return arrangements are to be effected;

- any necessary precautionary measures to reduce the risk of flight by the abductor with the child after the return order is made.

In most jurisdictions, the Central Authority is not directly involved in enforcement of return orders, but it will work co-operatively with other agencies and personnel to assist the enforcement process.

Legislative enforcement provisions already in effect include:[76]

- measures for the immediate execution of final orders;[77]

- directions for specific return arrangements to be made;[78]

---

[71] Germany, France, USA.
[72] United Kingdom, Australia.
[73] Canada: Quebec (s 10), Finland (s 35(2)), Germany (s 3(1)), New Zealand (s 9(1)). In several countries, it could also be possible to apply to the population register for information, including, *inter alia*, in Sweden, Germany and France.
[74] USA.
[75] Finland, Australia.
[76] The full title of each Act or Statue referred to is listed in Guide to Good Practice, Part II - Implementing Measures.
[77] Finland (s 46), Italy (art. 7(4)), United States (§§ 11601 *et seq.*).

- ▪ measures to prevent the child's re-abduction pending return;

- ▪ punitive measures to discourage avoidance of a return order;[79]

- ▪ authority for coercive detention or use of force;[80]

- ▪ issue of a warrant for the apprehension or detention of the child.[81]

Enforcement issues are dealt with in more detail in the Guide to Good Practice, Part II - Implementing Measures, Chapter 6.7.

The Permanent Bureau will also produce a report on enforcement issues, in accordance with recommendations from the Special Commission concerning the *Hague Convention of 25 October 1980 on the Civil Aspects of International Child Abduction* (27 September to 1 October 2002), with a view to the future publication of a Guide to Good Practice.

---

[78] Australia (Reg 20(1)).
[79] Sweden, Canada, Ireland, United Kingdom, USA.
[80] Germany (ANCJ s 33 and SorgeRÜbkAG s 8).
[81] Australia (reg 14), Canada: Quebec (s 10), Ireland (s 37), New Zealand (reg 26(1)), Sweden (s 19).

APPENDICES

LIST OF APPENDICES

APPENDIX 1

CONCLUSIONS AND RECOMMENDATIONS OF SPECIAL COMMISSION MEETINGS OF 1989, 1993, 1997, 2001, 2002

1989

CONCLUSIONS ON THE MAIN POINTS
DISCUSSED BY THE SPECIAL COMMISSION

adopted on 26 October 1989

I   There was broad consensus that in general the Convention works well in the interests of children and meets the needs for which it was drafted.

II   Nonetheless, it was recognized that considerable further effort had to be made in order to promote fuller understanding of the Convention on the part of judges, lawyers and administrative authorities, as well as parents and other persons exercising responsibility for children.

III   In light of the fundamental difficulties of a structural, legal and procedural nature encountered by States Parties in the handling by Spain of incoming requests for the return of children during the two years since the Convention entered into force for that country, Spain is strongly encouraged without further delay to take all appropriate measures to ensure that its Central Authority and its judicial and administrative authorities are provided the necessary powers and adequate resources to enable it fully to comply with its obligations under the Convention.

IV   Moreover, the Special Commission encourages States, whether contemplating becoming Parties to the Convention or already Parties, to organize their legal and procedural structures in such a way as to ensure the effective operation of the Convention and to give their Central Authorities adequate powers to play a dynamic role, as well as the qualified personnel and resources, including modern means of communication, needed in order expeditiously to handle requests for return of children or for access.

V   Central Authorities, in seeking to locate children within their territories, should be able to obtain information from other governmental agencies and authorities and to communicate such information to interested persons. Where necessary, their enquiries should be exempted from legislation or regulations concerning the confidentiality of such information.

VI   The Special Commission saw a correlation between the obligations of Central Authorities under Article 7 *f* to assist in the initiation of court proceedings for return of a child and the reservation under Article 26 concerning lawyers' fees, made by a number of States. Countries with broad territories and either no legal aid system or territorially non-unified legal aid had experienced or might experience in the future difficulties in obtaining legal representation for applicants who could not afford legal fees. The Special Commission encourages such States to intensify their efforts to obtain legal counsel or advisers in order to avoid serious prejudice to the interests of the children involved.

VII   The Special Commission agreed that periodic meetings on the operation of the Convention would be particularly useful as a means of improving the co-operation and effectiveness of Central Authorities and would thereby help to ensure the appropriate operation and implementation of the Convention. It recommends therefore that the Secretary General convene a second session of the Special Commission before 1993.

1993

**REPORT OF THE SECOND SPECIAL COMMISSION MEETING
TO REVIEW THE OPERATION OF THE HAGUE CONVENTION
ON THE CIVIL ASPECTS OF INTERNATIONAL CHILD ABDUCTION**
(18-21 JANUARY 1993)

PART TWO:

CONCLUSIONS ON CERTAIN IMPORTANT POINTS DISCUSSED BY THE SPECIAL COMMISSION

Conclusion 1   The Convention works well in practice and the States Parties are generally happy with its operation. Nonetheless, improvement can be made in a number of areas.

Conclusion 2   The key concepts which determine the scope of the Convention are not dependent for their meaning on any single legal system. Thus the expression "rights of custody", for example, does not coincide with any particular concept of custody in a domestic law, but draws its meaning from the definitions, structure and purposes of the Convention.

Conclusion 3   The Central Authorities designated by the States Parties play a key role in making the Convention function. They should act dynamically and should be provided with the staff and other resources needed in order to carry out their functions effectively.

Conclusion 4   Children who have been wrongfully removed or retained abroad are to be returned promptly, according to the Convention. Central Authorities should acknowledge receipt of an application immediately and endeavour to provide follow-up information rapidly. Practical arrangements for the safe return of children should be under contemplation from the commencement of the application.

Conclusion 5   Access to children is a normal counterpart to rights of custody. It would be desirable to have more information about the ultimate arrangements made for the exercise of access following the wrongful removal or retention of a child, both in cases where the child has been returned and in cases where return has been refused.

Conclusion 6   Interpol can play a constructive and helpful role in locating abducted children. It is not necessary to institute criminal proceedings in order to seek such help, which may be obtained on the basis of a missing persons report, and indeed criminal proceedings may be counter-productive in particular cases. Central Authorities of a number of countries systematically discourage the institution of such proceedings. It is up to each country to determine what use could be made of the INTERPOL communications network, in connection with child abductions.

Conclusion 7   Delay in legal proceedings is a major cause of difficulties in the operation of the Convention. All possible efforts should be made to expedite such proceedings. Courts in a number of countries normally decide on requests for return of a child on the basis only of the application and any documents or statements in writing submitted by the parties, without taking oral testimony or requiring the presence of the parties in person. This can serve to expedite the disposition of the case. The decision to return the child is not a decision on the merits of custody.

Conclusion 8   Due to the reservation taken under Article 26 of the Convention and the lack of a comprehensive legal aid system, the problem of obtaining practising lawyers to handle applications on a *pro bono* basis in the United States of America remains a hindrance to the rapid and efficient operation of the Convention in a significant number of cases where the United States is the requested State. This problem arises when the applicant cannot afford attorney's fees, except in the States of California and Washington where the Attorney General's office and local public prosecutors act as the intermediary of the United States Central Authority under Article 7 *f* of the Hague Convention. The Central Authority in the United States is continuing its efforts to assist in obtaining attorneys willing to act *pro bono* and efforts are beginning within the local bar associations in the other States to alleviate this problem.

Conclusion 9   The Permanent Bureau cannot, with its present resources, monitor all of the case law under the Convention in the different States Parties and communicate this case law to the Central Authorities and to practising lawyers. The Permanent Bureau, however, should make an effort to collect the most significant decisions handed down by the courts and, where possible, communicate the essential aspects of these to the Central Authorities. For this purpose, a standard form was envisaged which Central Authorities might use in reporting court decisions to the Permanent Bureau.[82] This effort did not preclude that the Central Authorities might also send copies of routine court decisions to the Permanent Bureau for collection and ultimate use for statistical purposes.

Conclusion 10   The work done by the Permanent Bureau and the discussions held by the Special Commission are of continuing importance to the effective operation of the Convention. The Special Commission should be convened periodically to study the application of the Convention in practice.

Following the Checklist of issues to be considered at the second meeting of the Special Commission (Prel. Doc. No 1), adopted by the Special Commission as its agenda, the Report on the issues posed by the Checklist is as set out below:

---

[82] NB: Subsequent to the Special Commission meeting the Permanent Bureau drafted a standard form for this purpose and circulated it to the Central Authorities for comment.

1997

Extracts of the Report of the third Special Commission meeting to review the operation of the Hague Convention on the Civil Aspects of International Child Abduction
(17-21 March 1997)

drawn up by the Permanent Bureau

INTRODUCTION

ANNEX I   Working Document No 3 distributed 17 March 1997 - Document submitted by the delegation of Australia.

ANNEX II   Working Document No 20 distributed 20 March 1997 - Document submitted by the delegations of Australia, Monaco, New Zealand, Norway, Sweden, Switzerland and the United Kingdom.

ANNEX III   Synthetic Revision of Working Document No 20, as drawn up by the Permanent Bureau in the light of comments and suggestions made by experts.

INTRODUCTION

The Special Commission studying the operation of the *Convention of 25 October 1980 on the Civil Aspects of International Child Abduction* held its third meeting at the Peace Palace 17-21 March 1997. Of the 42 States represented, 35 were Parties to the Convention under study (six being non-Members of the Conference) and the other seven Member States of the Hague Conference which were not yet Parties to the Convention. Six additional States, non-Members of the Conference, participated as observers. Thirty-two Member States and thirteen non-Member States, totalling forty-five, were Parties to the Convention at the time of this meeting.

Intergovernmental organisations represented by observers included the United Nations Committee on the Rights of the Child, the Commonwealth Secretariat, the Council of Europe and the European Parliament. International non-governmental organisations represented included the International Bar Association, International Social Service, the International Society of Family Law, the International Association of Juvenile and Family Court Magistrates, the International Union of Latin Notaries, Defence for Children International and the International Academy of Matrimonial Lawyers.

Mr P.H. Pfund, Delegate of the United States, was elected Chairman of the Special Commission, while Mrs A. Borrás, Delegate of Spain, was elected Vice-Chair. The Permanent Bureau served as Reporter for the Special Commission.

The documents on which the Commission based its work were as follows:

–   Preliminary Document No 1: Checklist of issues to be considered at the third meeting of the Special Commission, drawn up by the Permanent Bureau;

–   Preliminary Document No 2: Statistics submitted by the Governments;

–   Preliminary Document No 3: Bibliography.

The discussions ranged over a broad group of issues posed in the Checklist and the responses to the issues posed are reflected in a question-by-question report, which follows this introduction. Twenty-four working documents were submitted and of these two, which were the subject of detailed discussion, have been included as annexes to the Report. The following Report has been drawn up by the Permanent Bureau, which was asked to do so by the Special Commission.

ANNEX I

Working Document No 3
distributed 17 March 1997

Document submitted by the delegation of Australia

Background to the proposal

At the Special Commission meeting on General Affairs in 1995 Australia proposed that consideration be given to the ways in which the welfare of children could be protected when returning to their country of habitual residence. A copy of that proposal is attached.

In that proposal, two suggestions were made:

1   a proposal that State parties to the Convention accept that the Central Authority in each country has a responsibility to protect the welfare of children returned to that country;

2   a proposal for formal recognition by State parties to the Convention of the practice that has developed of courts requiring undertakings from applicants as a condition of ordering the return of a child.

Australia now seeks the support of other States to consider whether Central Authorities should accept a wider role of protecting the welfare of children on return under the Convention.

Reasons in support of the proposal

Such a role could be based on the current cooperation arrangements under the Hague Convention being extended beyond the securing of a court order for return of a child. It is not proposed that Central Authorities should be occupied with all cases beyond this point, but merely those cases where issues relating to the welfare of the child (*e.g.* allegations of child abuse) have been raised during the proceedings for the return on the child. In such cases, the Central Authority of the returning country would provide this information to the Central Authority of the requesting country, which would ensure appropriate measures to protect the welfare of the child on return.

This level of assistance could be said to fall well within Article 7 *h)* which states that parties shall take all appropriate measures "to provide such administrative arrangements as may be necessary and appropriate to secure the safe return of the child". The words used are "safe return" not simply "return" which arguably involves an obligation on the part of both States going beyond the mere safe transportation of the child to the requesting State. The Full Court of The Family Court of Australia (3 judges) stated in the case of *Cooper* v. *Casey* (1995) *FLC* 92-575 that there is an obligation on Central Authorities to protect returning children. The New Zealand Court of Appeal found a similar duty existed in the case of *Andersen* v. *Central Authority* for New Zealand (23 May 1995). Similarly, in the recent case of *Bell* v. *Bell* (23 December 1996), the Superior Court of California ordered the return of a child from California to Australia, the child to be returned to the care of welfare authorities in the state of Queensland pending a decision of the Family Court as to where the child should live.

Australian courts apply the Convention very strictly and in the majority of cases children are returned to the requesting country. To date the Family Court of Australia has taken a strong line in decisions under the Convention that issues relating to child abuse, violence against an abducting parent, financial support and accommodation must be left to the courts and government authorities of the requesting State on return. Unless agreement is reached with other parties to the Convention on measures to ensure that appropriate protection is in fact provided on return, it is likely that pressures will grow on the Court and the Australian Government to take a different approach to the issue. There is anecdotal evidence that courts in some countries are refusing to return children under the Convention for this reason.

Australian courts take the view that it is necessary in these situations to return the child to uphold the principles of the Convention, but that there should be safeguards in place to protect the returning parent and child.

However, in carrying out their obligations under the Convention, the Australian Government and courts face increasing criticism that the Convention does not provide measures for the physical and financial protection of abducting parents and children where children are returned under the Convention and that parents and children returning to their countries of habitual residence do not have adequate protection from violence, adequate financial support and adequate access to legal representation. In the future it may well be that the Australian community will no longer accept that abducting parents should be left to deal with these issues as best they can on return.

Although Central Authorities will not usually be in a position to directly provide services to returning parents, they could assume responsibility to provide contact numbers for services or assist returning parents to contact those services.

The Australian Central Authority now provides an information sheet of addresses and phone numbers of all legal and welfare services available to a returning parent. The parent can then contact those services direct, or the Central Authority can liaise between the parent and the service provider.

Australia does not wish to deter future accessions to the Convention by raising too high the level of what is expected of Central Authorities. However, we do not consider that the compilation of a list of services available in the requested country in an onerous responsibility for Central Authorities.

Acceptance of Australia's proposal will give formal recognition to an existing practice, which has developed between some countries that where a returning parent has fears for her physical safety and welfare, but a return cannot be refused (because the exception to return in Article 13 *b)* cannot be established because there may be no harm to the child), then Central Authorities are asked to assist as much as possible to facilitate the safe return of the parent and child.

It has been said that if Australian courts have such serious concerns for the welfare of returning parents and children, then the children should not be returned. This attitude defeats the purpose of the Convention and ignores two important considerations. One is that the first words of the Convention are that Contracting States are "Firmly convinced that the interests of children are of paramount importance in matters relating to their custody". The second is that it is an underlying principle of the Convention that children should be returned so that matters of custody and access can be resolved in the country of habitual residence. The child's best interests are not protected by this Convention if the abducting parent cannot safely return to participate effectively in a custody hearing.

Recommendation

1   that Contracting States agree to take responsibility for the welfare of returning children and parents to the extent permitted by the powers of their Central Authority and by the legal and social welfare system of their country. This responsibility can be read into the obligations imposed by Article 7 *h)*.

2   that as a minimum requirement, Central Authorities compile a list of legal and welfare services available to returning parents so that returning parents may contact those services direct.

Attachment to Working Document No 3
distributed 17 March 1997
Document submitted by the delegation of Australia

(Letter from the Attorney General's Department of April 1995)

The Australian Attorney-General's Department presents its compliments to the Permanent Bureau of the Hague Conference on Private International Law and refers to the Bureau's note dated 18 November 1994 requesting proposals for inclusion in the agenda for future work of the Conference.

The Australian Government proposes that a meeting be held of State parties to the Convention on the Civil Aspects of International Child Abduction to discuss measures to protect the welfare of children returned under the Convention to their country of habitual residence.

The operation of the Convention has come under scrutiny in Australia and other countries because of criticism that it does not provide measures for the physical and financial protection of abducting parents and children where children are returned under the Convention. In carrying out their obligations under the Convention, the Australian Central Authorities are increasingly faced with the difficulty of establishing to the satisfaction of the courts and the Australian community that parents and children returning to their countries of habitual residence will have adequate protection from violence, adequate financial support and adequate access to legal representation. The Australian Government is concerned that the Convention not become undermined by a reluctance to return children where such concerns exist.

The Australian Government notes two possible responses to this concern:

• arrangements for co-operation under the Hague Convention be extended to provide for

  - the provision, by the Central Authority of the requesting State to the Central Authority of the requested State, of information about issues relating to the welfare of the child raised during proceedings for the return of the child and

  - the acceptance of an obligation by the Central Authority of the requesting State to take steps to protect the welfare of the child on return;

  The Australian Government notes that, at least as an interim measure, such a response might be considered to be a measure to secure the safe return of the child as referred to in Article 7 *h)* of the Convention.

• formal recognition by State parties to the Convention of the practice that has developed of courts requiring undertakings from applicants as a condition of ordering the return of a child.

  The Australian Government notes that such measures might be considered to be consistent with the Convention where they enable a State party to return a child where it would otherwise not order the return of the child on a ground set down in Article 13 of the Convention or where such measures are temporary and aimed at the safe return of the child.

The Australian Attorney-General's Department avails itself of this opportunity to renew to the Bureau assurances of its highest consideration and esteem.

CANBERRA, April 1995.

ANNEX II

Working Document No 20
distributed 20 March 1997

Document submitted by the delegations of Australia, the United Kingdom, Monaco, New Zealand, Norway, Sweden and Switzerland

Working Document No 3 sets out a proposal by the delegation of Australia on ways in which the welfare of children can be protected when returning to the country of habitual residence.

Following discussion of Australia's proposal, delegations appeared to accept the following proposals:

1   It is essential to the integrity of the Convention to ensure the safety of children on their return to their country of habitual residence, in order to avoid both adverse public reaction and a reluctance of judges to order the return of children where issues of abuse or violence arise.

2   An increase in the number of refusals to return, in cases where such issues arise, would not be desirable. Accordingly, a narrow interpretation of Article 13 *b)* of the Convention should be encouraged by strengthening the role of Central Authorities in co-operating to protect children and parents on return. It is recognised that the ability of Central Authorities to take action to protect returning children and parents is limited by each Contracting State's system of domestic law and administrative arrangements. Central Authorities should, nevertheless, be prepared and encouraged by their respective States to adopt a flexible approach to their obligations under Article 7 *h)* of the Convention.

Conclusions

In view of the above proposals, delegations are urged to adopt the following conclusions:

1   To the extent permitted by the powers of their Central Authority and by the legal and social welfare systems of their country, Contracting States accept that Central Authorities have an obligation under Article 7 *h)* to protect the welfare of children upon return until the jurisdiction of the appropriate court has been effectively invoked.

2   It is recognised that the child's best interests are not protected by this Convention if the abducting parent cannot safely return to participate effectively in a custody hearing. Central Authorities should therefore also co-operate to the fullest extent possible to assist and protect returning parents.

3   The measures which may be taken in fulfilment of these obligations will vary according to the circumstances of each particular case. They may include, for example:

a   alerting the appropriate protection agencies or judicial authorities in the requesting State of the return of a child who may be in danger;

b   advising the requested State of the protective measures available in the requesting State to secure the safe return of a particular child;

c   providing the requested State with a report on the welfare of the child after return;

d   encouraging the use of Article 21 of the Convention to secure the effective exercise of access or visitation rights.

ANNEX III

Synthetic revision of Working Document No 20
as drawn up by the Permanent Bureau in the light of comments and suggestions made by experts

Working Document No 3 sets out a proposal by the delegation of Australia on ways in which the welfare of children can be protected when returning to the country of habitual residence.

Following discussion of Australia's proposal, delegations appeared to accept the following proposals:

1   It is essential to the integrity of the Convention to ensure the safety of children on their return to their country of habitual residence, in order to alleviate possible concerns and the reluctance of judges to order the return of children where issues of (alleged) abuse or violence arise.

2   An increase in the number of refusals to return, in cases where such issues arise, would not be desirable. Accordingly, a narrow interpretation of Article 13 *b)* of the Convention should be encouraged by strengthening the role of Central Authorities in co-operating to facilitate awareness of government or public resources available to parents and children. In that context, Central Authorities should be prepared and encouraged by their respective States to adopt a flexible approach to their obligations under Article 7 *h)* of the Convention.

Conclusions

In view of the above proposals, delegations are urged to adopt the following conclusions:

1   To the extent permitted by the powers of their Central Authority and by the legal and social welfare systems of their country, Contracting States accept that Central Authorities have an obligation under Article 7 *h)* to ensure appropriate child protection bodies are alerted so they may act to protect the welfare of children upon return until the jurisdiction of the appropriate court has been effectively invoked, in certain cases.

2   It is recognised that, in most cases, a consideration of the child's best interests requires that both parents have the opportunity to participate and be heard in custody proceedings. Central Authorities should therefore co-operate to the fullest extent possible to provide information respecting, legal, financial, protection and other resources in the requesting State, and facilitate contact with these bodies in appropriate cases.

[3-   The measures which may be taken in fulfilment of the obligation under Article 7 *h)* to take or cause to be taken an action to protect the welfare of children may include, for example:

a   alerting the appropriate protection agencies or judicial authorities in the requesting State of the return of a child who may be in danger;

b   advising the requested State, upon request, of the protective measures and services available in the requesting State to secure the safe return of a particular child;

[*c*   providing the requested State with a report on the welfare of the child;]

d   encouraging the use of Article 21 of the Convention to secure the effective exercise of access or visitation rights.]

Note by the Permanent Bureau

The delegation of Italy agreed with the suggested changes regarding Conclusion 1. The Italian experts did not object to the wording of Conclusions 2 and 3. They suggested, regarding Conclusion 3, that one item be added, to provide that applications for return, should include, whenever possible, a description of the services or measures available in the requesting State for the protection of the child or the returning parent. The delegation of Austria with respect to Conclusion 2 preferred the wording suggested in Working Document No 20 to that suggested by the Canadian experts. In addition, the Austrian experts wished Conclusion 2 to specify that returning parents should be given assistance even when *ex parte* custody orders have been issued after the abduction and that such orders should not prejudge the final outcome of the proceedings. The experts also wished that Conclusion 3 *c*, be deleted and that it be clearly stated, under Conclusion 3 *b*, that information was only required upon request. The delegation of France, with respect to Conclusions 1 and 2, reminded the meeting that the French Central Authority could not ensure that custody proceedings would be instituted upon return, although it could commit to assist the parent in all possible ways, in particular by contacting other authorities or services. The French experts found Conclusion 3 to be too specific and would prefer it more open-ended. Regarding Conclusion 3 *c*, it was pointed out that the French Central Authority could not provide information beyond the measures taken upon the return, for it lacked the resources needed for a long-term follow-up. Other experts expressed similar concerns as those mentioned above, including those regarding Conclusions 3 *b* and 3 *c*. Experts also wished that it be made clear that the purpose of the proposal was to protect the child and not to reward the abducting parent.

The square brackets around Conclusion No 3 reflect the doubts of certain experts as to whether this provision should be retained and the internal square brackets around sub-paragraph *c* reflect particular doubt as to the acceptability of this provision.

2001

**Conclusions and Recommendations of the Fourth Meeting of the Special Commission to Review the Operation of the Hague Convention of 25 October 1980 on the Civil Aspects of International Child Abduction
(22–28 March 2001)**

drawn up by the Permanent Bureau

TABLE OF CONTENTS

PART VI - CROSS FRONTIER ACCESS/CONTACT

PART VII – MATTERS OF A GENERAL NATURE

- *The 1996 Hague Convention on Child Protection*
- *Encouraging further ratifications and accessions*
- *Decisions on relocation*

PART VIII – INCADAT, RESEARCH AND THE JUDGES' NEWSLETTER

- *The International Child Abduction Database (INCADAT)*
- *Research*
- *The Judges' Newsletter on International Child Protection*

GENERAL CONCLUSION

PART I - THE ROLE AND FUNCTIONS OF CENTRAL AUTHORITIES

Structural issues

1.1   The Central Authorities designated by the Contracting States play a key role in making the Convention function. They should be given a mandate which is sufficiently broad, and the qualified personnel and the resources, including modern means of communication, necessary to act dynamically and carry out their functions effectively. Central Authorities should have a regular staff, able to develop expertise in the operation of the Convention.

1.2   Contracting States should inform the Permanent Bureau promptly of the contact details of their Central Authority(ies), and Central Authorities should inform the Permanent Bureau promptly of the names of contact persons, of the means by which they may be contacted and of their languages of communication. Central Authorities should promptly inform the Permanent Bureau of any changes in these details.

Communication and co-operation in respect of individual cases

1.3   Central Authorities should acknowledge receipt of an application immediately and endeavour to provide follow-up information rapidly. Central Authorities should reply promptly to communications from other Central Authorities.

1.4   Central Authorities should, as far as possible, use modern rapid means of communication in order to expedite proceedings, bearing in mind the requirements of confidentiality.

1.5   In relation to the translation of documents, Central Authorities are reminded of the provisions of Article 24 of the Convention.

1.6   The requesting Central Authority should ensure that each application is accompanied by a sufficient statement of the legal and factual basis on which the application rests, in particular concerning the matters of the habitual residence of the child, rights of custody and the exercise of those rights, as well as detailed information on location of the child. Central Authorities are reminded of the model form for the Request for Return recommended by the Fourteenth Session of the Hague Conference (*Actes et Documents*, (Proceedings) *XIV ème Session*, p. 423, and on the Hague Conference website at: <http://www.hcch.net/e/conventions/expl28e.html>).

Exchange of information

1.7   Each Central Authority is encouraged, where this is feasible, to establish and regularly update a website, details of which should be furnished to the Permanent Bureau for the purpose of establishing a link with the Hague Conference website.

1.8   It is recommended that each Central Authority should publish, on its website if possible and/or by other means, such as a brochure or flyer (the precise format being a matter for the Central Authority), information concerning at least the following matters:

-    the other Contracting States in relation to whom the Convention is in effect;
-    the means by which a missing child may be located;
-    the designation and contact details for the Central Authority;
-    application procedures (for return and access), documentary requirements, any standard forms employed and any language requirements;
-    details, where applicable, of how to apply for legal aid or otherwise for the provision of legal service;

- the judicial procedures, including appeals procedures, which apply to return applications;
- enforcement options and procedures for return and access orders;
- any special requirements which may arise in the course of the proceedings (*e.g.* with regard to matters of evidence);
- information concerning the services applicable for the protection of a returning child (and accompanying parent, where relevant), and concerning applications for legal aid for, or the provision of legal services to, the accompanying parent on return;
- information, if applicable, concerning liaison judges.

Locating the child

1.9   Central Authorities, in seeking to locate children, should be able to obtain information from other governmental agencies and authorities and to communicate such information to interested authorities. Where possible, their enquiries should be exempted from legislation or regulations concerning the confidentiality of such information. Interpol can play a constructive and helpful role in locating abducted children.

Securing the voluntary return of the child

1.10   Contracting States should encourage voluntary return where possible. It is proposed that Central Authorities should as a matter of practice seek to achieve voluntary return, as intended by Article 7 *c)* of the Convention, where possible and appropriate by instructing to this end legal agents involved, whether state attorneys or private practitioners, or by referral of parties to a specialist organisation providing an appropriate mediation service. The role played by the courts in this regard is also recognised.

1.11   Measures employed to assist in securing the voluntary return of the child or to bring about an amicable resolution of the issues should not result in any undue delay in return proceedings.

1.12   Contracting States should ensure the availability of effective methods to prevent either party from removing the child prior to the decision on return.

Securing the safe return of the child

1.13   To the extent permitted by the powers of their Central Authority and by the legal and social welfare systems of their country, Contracting States accept that Central Authorities have an obligation under Article 7 *h)* to ensure appropriate child protection bodies are alerted so they may act to protect the welfare of children upon return in certain cases where their safety is at issue until the jurisdiction of the appropriate court has been effectively invoked.

It is recognised that, in most cases, a consideration of the child's best interests requires that both parents have the opportunity to participate and be heard in custody proceedings. Central Authorities should therefore co-operate to the fullest extent possible to provide information in respect of legal, financial, protection and other resources in the requesting State, and facilitate timely contact with these bodies in appropriate cases.

The measures which may be taken in fulfilment of the obligation under Article 7 *h)* to take or cause to be taken an action to protect the welfare of children may include, for example:

a   alerting the appropriate protection agencies or judicial authorities in the requesting State of the return of a child who may be in danger;

b   advising the requested State, upon request, of the protective measures and services available in the requesting State to secure the safe return of a particular child;

c encouraging the use of Article 21 of the Convention to secure the effective exercise of access or visitation rights.

It is recognised that the protection of the child may also sometimes require steps to be taken to protect an accompanying parent.

The maintenance of statistics

1.14 Central Authorities are encouraged to maintain accurate statistics concerning the cases dealt with by them under the Convention, and to make annual returns of statistics to the Permanent Bureau in accordance with the standard forms established by the Permanent Bureau in consultation with Central Authorities.

1.15 The Special Commission endorses the Permanent Bureau's plan to establish a statistical database as a complement to the International Child Abduction Database, and encourages Contracting States to consider methods by which the resources for the project may be made available.

Promoting good practices

1.16 Contracting States to the Convention should co-operate with each other and with the Permanent Bureau to develop a good practice guide which expands on Article 7 of the Convention. This guide would be a practical, "how-to" guide, to help implement the Convention. It would concentrate on operational issues and be targeted particularly at new Contracting States. It would not be binding nor infringe upon the independence of the judiciary. The methodology should be left to the Permanent Bureau.

PART II - SECURING STATE COMPLIANCE WITH CONVENTION OBLIGATIONS

Implementation

2.1 The national and regional legal frameworks, in which the Convention has to operate, are subject to sometimes significant changes. The same applies to technological means, which could potentially facilitate the operation of the Convention. It is therefore suggested that implementation, whether national or regional, should always be seen as a continuing process of development and improvement, even if the text of the Convention itself remains unchanged.

Standard questionnaire for newly-acceding States

2.2 In order to assist newly-acceding States to implement the Convention effectively, and to provide relevant information to existing Contracting States in considering whether to accept accessions in accordance with Article 38 of the Convention, the Special Commission gives its approval to a questionnaire to be addressed to newly acceding States, on the following understandings:

a that the Permanent Bureau would make the questionnaire available on the Hague Conference website and draw it to the attention of States which are known to be considering accession or which have recently acceded to the Convention;

b that it should be made clear that the provision of a response to the questionnaire is not compulsory but is recommended;

c that it would be for the State addressed to decide whether to communicate any response it makes through the Permanent Bureau to other Contracting States, or directly to such States as it may choose;

d   that existing Contracting States which have already acceded to the Convention might also use this facility, if they so wish, as a possible means of expediting the process of acceptance in their case.

2.3   The approved questionnaire is as follows:

I   *Implementing legislation*

(a)   *Is implementing legislation necessary to bring the Convention into force in domestic law?*
(b)   *If so, has the necessary legislation been enacted, and is it in force? (Please provide a copy or indicate where copies of the legislation may be obtained.)*

II   *Locating children*

Please indicate the agencies involved and the processes available for the location of missing children in your country.

III   *Central Authority*

(a)   *The designation and contact details of the Central Authority.*
(b)   *Contact persons within the Central Authority, languages spoken, contact details for each.*
(c)   *Please indicate measures taken to ensure that the Central Authority is in a position to carry out the functions set out in Article 7 of the Convention?*

IV   *Judicial procedures*

(a)   *Which courts/administrative bodies within your system have been given jurisdiction to consider applications for return orders (and questions of access) under the Convention?*
(b)   *What measures exist to ensure that return applications will be dealt with expeditiously at first instance and on appeal?*
(c)   *What facilities are available to foreign applicants to assist them in bringing their applications before the courts, and in particular is legal aid available and, if so, on what conditions?*

V   *Enforcement procedures*

What procedures and measures exist for the enforcement of:

(a)   *a return order?*
(b)   *a contact/access order?*

VI   *Substantive law*

(a)   *What are the legal criteria by which custody and contact determinations are made?*
(b)   *Is there a difference in the legal status of mothers and fathers in custody or contact cases?*

VII   *Social services and child protection services*

Please describe the services which exist for the assessment, care and protection of children in the context of international child abduction.

Please indicate the services available for the protection (if necessary) of returning children, as well as the services available (including legal advice and representation) to a parent accompanying the child on return.

VIII   *Information and training*

What measures are being taken to ensure that persons responsible for implementing the Convention (e.g. judges and Central Authority personnel) have received appropriate information and training? (Note: the Permanent Bureau may be contacted for information in relation to forms of assistance which may be available for this purpose.)

Monitoring and review

2.4   The Special Commission reaffirms the value of Special Commission meetings to review the operation of the Convention, and regards the four-year cycle for general reviews as satisfactory.

2.5   The Special Commission supports the holding of additional meetings to address specific issues when these are clearly shown to be necessary.

2.6   In order to enable less wealthy Contracting States to be represented at Special Commission meetings, the Secretary General should, when convoking a meeting, invite Contracting States to consider giving support to specific States or contributing to a common fund.

2.7   Established Central Authorities are encouraged to explore ways of sharing their expertise and experiences with other Central Authorities when requested to do so.

2.8   Central Authorities should explore mechanisms for improving the flow of information to the Permanent Bureau (and vice-versa) with a view to identifying and solving potential problems and assisting the process of monitoring.

2.9   Central Authorities are encouraged, in addressing any practical problems concerning the proper functioning of the Convention, to engage in dialogue with one another. Where a group of Central Authorities share a common problem, consideration should be given to joint meetings which might in some cases be facilitated by the Hague Conference.

2.10   The Special Commission notes the increase in recent years in the holding of judicial (and other) seminars and conferences at the national, regional and international levels and underlines the importance of such meetings and the contribution which they make to the development of the mutual understanding and confidence between judges necessary to support the effective functioning of the Convention.

PART III - JUDICIAL PROCEEDINGS, INCLUDING APPEALS AND ENFORCEMENT ISSUES, AND QUESTIONS OF INTERPRETATION

Courts organisation

3.1   The Special Commission calls upon Contracting States to bare in mind the considerable advantages to be gained by a concentration of jurisdiction to deal with Hague Convention cases within a limited number of courts.

3.2   The progress already made in certain Contracting States, as well as the consideration now being given to this matter in others, is welcomed. Where a concentration of jurisdiction is not possible, it is particularly important that judges concerned in proceedings be offered appropriate training or briefing.

Speed of Hague procedures, including appeals

3.3   The Special Commission underscores the obligation (Article 11) of Contracting States to process return applications expeditiously, and that this obligation extends also to appeal procedures.

3.4   The Special Commission calls upon trial and appellate courts to set and adhere to timetables that ensure the speedy determination of return applications.

3.5   The Special Commission calls for firm management by judges, both at trial and appellate levels, of the progress of return proceedings.

The provision of legal aid and advice

3.6   In States where an applicant for a return order is in effect unable to bring his/her application promptly before the courts in the requested State, this constitutes a serious hindrance to the rapid and efficient operation of the Convention. The Special Commission encourages such States to intensify their efforts to obtain legal counsel or advisers in order to avoid serious prejudice to the interests of the children involved.

Manner of taking evidence

3.7   Rules and practices concerning the taking and admission of evidence, including the evidence of experts, should be applied in return proceedings with regard to the necessity for speed and the importance of limiting the enquiry to the matters in dispute which are directly relevant to the issue of return.

Procedures for hearing the child, and determining whether the child objects to return

3.8   There are considerable differences of approach to the question of interviewing the child concerned. Some States have strong reservations about the appropriateness of interviewing young children in connection with return applications. Where it is appropriate and necessary to do so, it is desirable that the person interviewing the child should be properly trained or experienced and should shield the child from the burden of decision-making.

Methods and speed of enforcement

3.9   Delays in enforcement of return orders, or their non-enforcement, in certain Contracting States are matters of serious concern. The Special Commission calls upon Contracting States to enforce return orders promptly and effectively.

3.10   It should be made possible for courts, when making return orders, to include provisions to ensure that the order leads to the prompt and effective return of the child.

3.11   Efforts should be made by Central Authorities, or by other competent authorities, to track the outcome of return orders and to determine in each case whether enforcement is delayed or not achieved.

PART IV - INTERPRETATION OF KEY CONCEPTS

Approach to interpretation

4.1   The Convention should be interpreted having regard to its autonomous nature and in the light of its objects.

4.2   The Special Commission emphasises the continuing importance as an aid to the interpretation and understanding of the Convention of the Explanatory Report by Elisa Pérez-Vera, and notes the value of a recent translation of the Report into Spanish.

Article 13, paragraph 1 b)

4.3   The Article 13, paragraph 1 *b)*, "grave risk" defence has generally been narrowly construed by courts in the Contracting States, and this is confirmed by the relatively small number of return applications which were refused on this basis according to the Statistical Analysis of Applications made in 1999 (Prel. Doc. No 3, March 2001). It is in keeping with the objectives of the Convention, as confirmed in the Explanatory Report by Elisa Pérez-Vera (at paragraph 34), to interpret this defence in a restrictive fashion.

Consent and acquiescence (Article 13, paragraph 1 a))

4.4   Efforts to achieve an amicable resolution of the issues should not be construed as giving rise to acquiescence or consent.

Article 20

4.5   The Special Commission notes that there have been very few reported cases in which a return order has been refused on the basis of Article 20, and that no such cases were reported in the Statistical Analysis of Applications made in 1999 (Prel. Doc. No 3, March 2001).

PART V - ISSUES SURROUNDING THE SAFE AND PROMPT RETURN OF THE CHILD (AND THE CUSTODIAL PARENT, WHERE RELEVANT)

Safe return orders

5.1   Contracting States should consider the provision of procedures for obtaining, in the jurisdiction to which the child is to be returned, any necessary provisional protective measures prior to the return of the child.

Criminal proceedings

5.2   The impact of a criminal prosecution for child abduction on the possibility of achieving a return of the child is a matter which should be capable of being taken into account in the exercise of any discretion which the prosecuting authorities have to initiate, suspend or withdraw charges.

Immigration matters

5.3   Contracting States should, as far as possible, take measures to ensure that, save in exceptional cases, the abducting parent will be permitted to enter the Country to which the child is returned for the purpose of taking part in legal proceedings concerning custody or protection of the child.

The provision of legal aid and advice

5.4   Contracting States should take measures to ensure that parents who participate in custody proceedings after a child's return are given adequate access to a country's legal system to adequately present their case.[1]

---

[1] States are reminded of the *Hague Convention of 25 October 1980 on International Access to Justice*, which *inter alia* generalizes the principles of Article 25 of the Child Abduction Convention.

Direct judicial communications

5.5   Contracting States are encouraged to consider identifying a judge or judges or other persons or authorities able to facilitate at the international level communications between judges or between a judge and another authority.

5.6   Contracting States should actively encourage international judicial co-operation. This takes the form of attendance of judges at judicial conferences by exchanging ideas/communications with foreign judges or by explaining the possibilities of direct communication on specific cases.

        In Contracting States in which direct judicial communications are practised, the following are commonly accepted safeguards:

        -       communications to be limited to logistical issues and the exchange of information;
        -       parties to be notified in advance of the nature of proposed communication;
        -       record to be kept of communications;
        -       confirmation of any agreement reached in writing;
        -       parties or their representatives to be present in certain cases, for example via conference call facilities.

5.7   The Permanent Bureau should continue to explore the practical mechanisms for facilitating direct international judicial communications.

PART VI - CROSS FRONTIER ACCESS/CONTACT

6.1   The Special Commission recognises the deficiencies of the Convention in achieving the objective of securing protection for rights of access in transfrontier situations. This is regarded by Contracting States as a serious problem requiring urgent attention in the interests of the children and parents concerned.

6.2   The Special Commission recommends that the Permanent Bureau should carry out further consultations with Member States of the Hague Conference, as well as Contracting States to the 1980 Convention, on the basis of the Preliminary Report on "Transfrontier Access/Contact and the Hague Convention of 25 October 1980 on the Civil Aspects of International Child Abduction" (Prel. Doc. No 4 of March 2001) together with the Report (to be drawn up by the Permanent Bureau) on this Special Commission. The Permanent Bureau should proceed to the completion of the Final Report in accordance with the decision of the Special Commission on General Affairs and Policy of the Conference (8-12 May 2000). Other developments at the global and regional levels will be taken into account. The decision to be taken by the Commission on General Affairs and Policy of the Hague Conference (at the Nineteenth Session in June 2001) on the further steps which may be appropriate should reflect the serious nature of the problem and the need for urgent action.

PART VII – MATTERS OF A GENERAL NATURE

The 1996 Hague Convention on Child Protection

7.1   The Special Commission recognises the potential advantages of the *Hague Convention of 19 October 1996 on Jurisdiction, Applicable Law, Recognition, Enforcement and Co-operation in respect of Parental Responsibility and Measures for the Protection of Children* as an adjunct to the 1980 Convention, and recommends that Contracting States should consider ratification or accession.

Encouraging further ratifications and accessions

7.2 Endeavours should continue to be made to encourage ratifications of, and accessions to, the 1980 Convention by States willing and able to undertake the Convention obligations. Contracting States are encouraged to arrange meetings at the regional level for this purpose.

Decisions on relocation

7.3 Courts take significantly different approaches to relocation cases, which are occurring with a frequency not contemplated in 1980 when the Convention was drafted. It is recognised that a highly restrictive approach to relocation applications may have an adverse effect on the operation of the 1980 Convention.

PART VIII – INCADAT, RESEARCH AND THE JUDGES' NEWSLETTER

The International Child Abduction Database (INCADAT)

8.1 The Special Commission welcomes with enthusiasm the establishment by the Permanent Bureau of the International Child Abduction Database and congratulates all those responsible for its development. INCADAT will be of significant assistance to the judiciary, Central Authorities, the legal profession, as well as individuals affected by or interested in child abduction. Contracting States are encouraged to collaborate with the Permanent Bureau to explore possible sources of funding (including partnership funding) or material assistance to assist in the completion of INCADAT and to secure its position for the future.

Research

8.2 The Special Commission recognises the value of research, including socio-legal research, into the operation of the Convention and into the outcomes of cases dealt with under the Convention. It records its appreciation to the authors of Preliminary Document No 3 "A Statistical Analysis of Applications made in 1999 under the Hague Convention of 25 October 1980 on the Civil Aspects of International Child Abduction".

The Judges' Newsletter on International Child Protection

8.3 The Special Commission supports the publication and circulation by the Permanent Bureau of the Judges' Newsletter on International Child Protection.

GENERAL CONCLUSION

The Special Commission recognises that the Convention in general continues to work well in the interests of children and broadly meets the needs for which it was drafted.

2002

Conclusions and Recommendations of the Special Commission concerning the Hague Convention of 25 October 1980 on the Civil Aspects of International Child Abduction

(27 September to 1 October 2002)

1. **GOOD PRACTICE GUIDE**

    (a) Publication: The Permanent Bureau is authorised, in preparing the Guide to Good Practice for publication, to make changes of an editorial nature, to update, where necessary, any factual information contained in the Guide, to determine the presentation of the material in the Guide, provided that this did not involve any changes in substance or emphasis and to prepare a general introduction to the Guide explaining its background.

    (b) Preventive measures: The Permanent Bureau should continue to gather information concerning the measures adopted in different Contracting States to prevent abductions from taking place. The experience of non-governmental organisations in this field should be taken into account. The Permanent Bureau should prepare a report on the subject with a view to the possible development of a Guide to Good Practice.

    (c) Enforcement: The Permanent Bureau should continue to gather information on the practice of the enforcement of return orders in different Contracting States. The Permanent Bureau should prepare a report on the subject with a view to the possible development of a Guide to Good Practice.

2. **TRANSFRONTIER ACCESS / CONTACT**

    (a) It is premature to begin work on a Protocol to the 1980 Convention. If the alternative steps outlined below do not lead to significant improvements in practice, the issue of a Protocol should be revisited in the future.

    (b) Chapter 5 of Preliminary Document No 3 should be retained subject to agreed modifications.

    (c) Work should continue on a separate chapter of the Guide to Good Practice relating to transfrontier access/contact in the context of the 1980 Convention with the following objectives:
        a. to promote consistent and best practices in relation to those matters which it is agreed fall within the competence and obligations of States Parties under the Convention,
        b. to provide examples of practice even in relation to matters which fall within the disputed areas of interpretation.

    (d) Work should begin on the formulation of general principles and considerations. The idea is not to create a set of principles applying to access cases generally, but rather to draw attention to certain general considerations and special features, which need to be borne in mind by Contracting States and their authorities when formulating policies in respect of international access / contact cases. These general principles would not be binding; they would be advisory in nature. As well as offering general advice to States in formulating policy in this area, the general principles could be helpful to Central Authorities in informing their practice, they could possibly be helpful to the courts and other authorities, as well as to applicants as they present their cases.

(e)   It is recognised that the provisions of the Hague Convention of 19 October 1996 on Jurisdiction, Applicable Law, Recognition, Enforcement and Co-operation in respect of Parental Responsibility and Measures for the Protection of Children has the potential to make a substantial contribution to the solution of certain problems surrounding cross-frontier access/contact. Those States which have already agreed in principle to ratify or accede to the 1996 Convention are urged to proceed to ratification or accession with all due speed. Other States are strongly encouraged to consider the advantages of ratification or accession and implementation.

(f)   The Meeting notes and welcomes the readiness of some judges from common law jurisdictions to tackle problems posed by conflicting interpretations of Article 21 in their jurisprudence by proposing a common law judicial congress.

3.   CHILD ABDUCTION, TRANSFRONTIER ACCESS / CONTACT AND ISLAMIC STATES

The Permanent Bureau should continue the work it has begun concerning the development of co-operation between Islamic and other States in resolving problems of child abduction and transfrontier access/contact, including the analysis and review of the various bilateral agreements and arrangements that exist and exploration of the potential of a multilateral approach, including through the use of existing Hague Conventions.

4.   JUDICIAL SEMINARS AND THE JUDGES' NEWSLETTER

The meetings of judges from different jurisdictions foster international understanding, they promote judicial co-operation and they help to spread helpful practices and precedents across jurisdictions. The Hague Conference should continue to remain active in this area, providing assistance where it is requested, supporting the development of judicial co-operation and communications, both generally and in the context of individual cases where required, and continuing publication of Judges' Newsletters on International Child Protection.

5.   PRACTICAL MECHANISMS FOR FACILITATING DIRECT INTERNATIONAL JUDICIAL COMMUNICATIONS IN THE CONTEXT OF THE HAGUE CONVENTION OF 25 OCTOBER 1980 ON THE CIVIL ASPECTS OF INTERNATIONAL CHILD ABDUCTION

The Permanent Bureau will:

(a)   Continue the formal consultation with Member States of the Hague Conference as well as other States Parties to the 1980 Hague Convention, based on the Preliminary Report together with the Report that will be drawn up by the Permanent Bureau on the Conclusions and Recommendations of the Special Commission of September / October 2002.

(b)   Continue informal consultations with interested judges based on the Preliminary Report together with the Report that will be drawn up by the Permanent Bureau on the Conclusions and Recommendations of the Special Commission of September / October 2002.

(c)   Continue to examine the practical mechanisms and structures of a network of contact points to facilitate at the international level communications between judges or between a judge and another authority.

(d)   Complete the Final Report that will include further analysis of policy issues and tentative conclusions.

(e)   Draw up an inventory of existing practices relating to direct judicial communications in specific cases under the 1980 Hague Convention with the advice of a consultative group of experts drawn primarily from the judiciary.

6.   INCASTAT

With regard to the development of a database on the 1980 Hague Convention, the Meeting recognises the work begun by the Permanent Bureau, with the support of the Canadian Government and the WorldReach Software Corporation. It encourages the Permanent Bureau to continue these efforts in co-operation with Contracting States and their Central Authorities.

The Hague, 20 April 2001

APPENDIX 2

OBLIGATIONS ON CENTRAL AUTHORITIES

OBLIGATIONS ON CENTRAL AUTHORITIES

The obligations described here are arranged according to Convention Articles.

1   Implement objects expeditiously (Article 1 & 2)

Central Authorities must implement the objects of the Convention as expeditiously as possible. The objects of the Convention are:

a)   to secure the prompt return of children; and
b)   to ensure that rights of custody and of access are respected (*Article 1*).

2   Co-operate with other Central Authorities (Article 7)

Central Authorities must co-operate with each other to secure the prompt return of children and to achieve the other objects of the Convention;

They must also promote co-operation between their own domestic or national authorities and agencies to secure the prompt return of children and to achieve the other objects of the Convention;

Central Authorities must take all appropriate measures –

a)   to locate a child;
b)   to prevent further harm to the child or prejudice to interested parties;
c)   to secure the voluntary return of the child or to resolve matters amicably;
d)   to exchange information about the child's the social background;
e)   to provide information about the relevant laws of their country;
f)   to ensure that legal or other proceedings are commenced to obtain the return of the child;
ff)   to make arrangements for organizing or securing the effective exercise of rights of access;
g)   to ensure that applicants have access to legal aid and advice, or legal representation;
h)   to provide assistance to secure the safe return of the child;
i)   to keep each other informed about the operation of this Convention;
ii)   to eliminate any obstacles to the application of the Convention.

3   Applications for return (Article 8)

Central Authorities must receive and send applications for the return of abducted children.

The application must contain information about:

-       the applicant;
-       the child;
-       the abductor;
-       the legal and Convention grounds on which the applicant's claim for return of the child is based;
-       all available information about where and with whom the child is living or hiding.

4   Child no longer in the requested territory (Article 9)

If a child is no longer in the territory of the requested Contracting State, the Central Authority should promptly transmit the application to another Central Authority where the child is thought to be.

5   Voluntary return is desirable (Article 10)

Central Authorities must take all appropriate measures to obtain the voluntary return of the child.

6   Act expeditiously in proceedings (Articles 11; 2)

Central Authorities must act expeditiously in proceedings for the return of children.

7   Rights of access (Article 21)

Central Authorities must promote the peaceful enjoyment of access rights.

They must also take steps to remove all obstacles to the exercise of access rights.

8   Reasons for rejecting application (Article 27)

Central Authorities must inform the applicant or the requesting Central Authority of the reasons for rejecting an application for return.

APPENDIX 3

SAMPLE FORMS

Appendix 3.1
Return Request Form
(Paragraph 1.4.1)

**APPLICATION IN ACCORDANCE WITH THE
HAGUE CONVENTION ON THE CIVIL ASPECTS OF INTERNATIONAL CHILD
ABDUCTION FOR THE RETURN OF A CHILD ABDUCTED**

REQUESTING CENTRAL AUTHORITY OR APPLICANT:	REQUESTED AUTHORITY:

Concerns the following child:...who will attain the age of 16 on .... 20.........

NOTE: The following particulars should be completed insofar as possible.

I   IDENTITY OF THE CHILD AND ITS PARENTS

1   CHILD

Name and first names: ....

Date of birth: ....

Place of birth: ....

Habitual residence before removal or retention: ....
....

Passport or identity card No., if any: ....

Description and photo, if possible (see annexes): ....

2   PARENTS

2.1   MOTHER

Name and first names: ....

Date of birth: ....

Place of birth:

Nationality: ....

Occupation: ....

Habitual residence: ....
....

Passport or identity card
No., if any: ....

2.2 FATHER:

Name and first names: ....

Date of birth: ....

Place of birth: ....

Nationality: ....

Occupation: ....

Habitual residence: ....

Passport or identity card
No., if any: ....

2.3 Date and place of marriage: ....

II REQUESTING INDIVIDUAL OR INSTITUTION (who actually exercised custody before the removal or retention)

3   Name and first names: ....

Nationality of individual applicant: ....

Occupation of individual applicant: ....

Address: ....
....

Passport or identity card
No., if any: ....

Relation to the child: ....

Name and address of legal adviser, if
any: ....

III PLACE WHERE THE CHILD IS THOUGHT TO BE

4.1   Information concerning the person
alleged to have removed or retained the
child: ....

Name and first names: ....

Date and place of birth,
if known: ....

Nationality, if known: ....

Occupation: ....

Last known address: ....

....

Passport or identity card No., if any: ....

Description and photo, if possible (see annexes): ....

4.2 Address of the child: ....

4.3 Other persons who might be able to supply additional information relating to the whereabouts of the child: ....

....

IV   TIME, PLACE, DATE AND CIRCUMSTANCES OF THE WRONGFUL REMOVAL OR RETENTION

....
....
....
....
....

V   FACTUAL OR LEGAL GROUNDS JUSTIFYING THE REQUEST

....
....
....
....
....

VI   CIVIL PROCEEDINGS IN PROGESS

....
....
....
....
....

VII   CHILD IS TO BE RETURNED TO:

(a)   Name and first names: ....

Date and place of birth: ....

Address: ....
                                  ....

Telephone number: ....

(b)   Proposed arrangements for
       return of the child: ....

VIII   OTHER REMARKS

....
....
....
....
....

IX   LIST OF DOCUMENTS ATTACHED*

....
....
....
....
....

I authorise the requested Central Authority and its agents to act on my behalf and to do all things reasonable and necessary in connection with this application.

Date...

Place...

Signature and/or stamp of the requesting Central Authority or applicant

....

---

* *e.g.* Certified copy of relevant decision or agreement concerning rights of custody or rights of access; certificate or affidavit as to the applicable law; information relating to the social background of the child; authorization empowering the Central Authority to act on behalf of applicant.

Appendix 3.2
Access Request Form
(Paragraph 1.4.1)

**APPLICATION FOR RIGHTS OF ACCESS IN ACCORDANCE WITH THE
HAGUE CONVENTION ON THE CIVIL ASPECTS OF INTERNATIONAL CHILD
ABDUCTION FOR THE RETURN OF A CHILD ABDUCTED**

REQUESTING CENTRAL AUTHORITY OR APPLICANT:	REQUESTED AUTHORITY:

Concerns the following child:...who will attain the age of 16 on .... 20........

NOTE: The following particulars should be completed insofar as possible.

I   IDENTITY OF THE CHILD AND ITS PARENTS

1   CHILD

Name and first names: ....

Date of birth: ....

Place of birth: ....

Habitual residence: ....
                                                       ....

Passport or identity card
No., if any: ....

Description and photo, if possible
(see annexes):   ....

2   PARENTS

2.1   MOTHER

Name and first names: ....

Date of birth: ....

Place of birth: ....

Nationality: ....

Occupation: ....

Habitual residence: ....

                                           ....

Passport or identity card
No., if any: ....

2.2   **FATHER:**

Name and first names: ....

Date and place of birth: ....

Nationality: ....

Occupation: ....

Habitual residence: ....

                                           ....

Passport or identity card
No., if any: ....

2.3   **Date and place of marriage:**   ....

II   REQUESTING INDIVIDUAL OR INSTITUTION

3   Name and first names: ....

Nationality of individual applicant: ....

Occupation of individual applicant: ....

Address: ....

                                           ....

Passport or identity card
No., if any: ....

Relation to the child: ....

Name and address of legal adviser, if
any: ....

III   PLACE WHERE THE CHILD IS THOUGHT TO BE

4.1   Information concerning the person
        alleged to have prevented the exercise
        of rights of access or denied the
        enjoyment of access: ....

        Name and first names: ....

Date and place of birth,
if known: ....

Nationality, if known: ....

Occupation: ....

Last known address: ....
....

Passport or identity card No., if
any: ....

Description and photo, if
possible (see annexes): ....

4.2   Address of the child: ....
....

4.3   Other persons who might be able to
        supply additional information relating
        to the whereabouts of the child: ....
....
....
....
....

**IV   CIRCUMSTANCES RELATING TO THE PREVENTION OF EXERCISE OF RIGHTS
        OF ACCESS**

....
....
....
....
....

V   FACTUAL OR LEGAL GROUNDS JUSTIFYING THE REQUEST

....
....
....
....
....

VI   CIVIL PROCEEDINGS IN PROGESS

....
....
....
....
....

VII   PROPOSED ARRANGEMENTS TO SECURE EXERCISE OF RIGHTS OF ACCESS

....
....
....
....
....

VIII   OTHER REMARKS

....
....
....
....
....

IX   LIST OF DOCUMENTS ATTACHED*

....
....
....
....
....

I authorise the Central Authority and its agents to act on my behalf and to do all things reasonable and necessary in connection with this application.

Date..

Place..

Signature and/or stamp of the requesting Central Authority or applicant

....

---

* e.g. Certified copy of relevant decision or agreement concerning rights of custody or rights of access; certificate or affidavit as to the applicable law; information relating to the social background of the child; authorization empowering the Central Authority to act on behalf of applicant.

Appendix 3.3
Acknowledgement Form Requesting
Additional Information
(Paragraph 4.4)

TELEFAX COVER LETTER

To: Ms/Mr
        [country] Central Authority
        FAX:

From: [case manager]
        International Division

Date:

RE: **New Hague Convention Case – [CASE NAME]   ]**

Number of Pages (including this one): 1

Dear Ms/Mr

In regards to the above-mentioned case, I thank you for forwarding the Hague application. I have opened the case and begun attempts to verify the children's location.

As you know, we will need the following items in order to complete the application and move forward with the Hague petition process:

(1)   The Hague application translated into English;
(2)   Copy of child's birth certificate translated into English;
(3)   Copy of marriage certificate translated into English;
(4)   Copies of relevant *court orders*: divorce, separation, or custody, with English translations;
(5)   Indication whether the applicant wishes to pursue voluntary return, keeping in mind the risk that abducting parent may flee his current location upon receipt of such a letter;
(6)   Indication whether the applicant requires pro bono assistance; if so, please attach completed Legal Assistance Questionnaire with required supporting documentation;
(7)   Indication whether applicant speaks English, for purposes of finding a suitable attorney;
(8)   Indication whether the applicant can travel to the US.

Thank you for your kind assistance in this matter.

Sincerely,

[case manager]
International Division

Appendix 3.4
Checklist of Convention Requirements
for Incoming Application
(Paragraph 4.5)

HAGUE ABDUCTION APPLICATION - INCOMING

RETURN REQUEST: CHECKLIST OF REQUIREMENTS FOR HAGUE ABDUCTION
CONVENTION

Application Received from : _____(country)

Administrative
[]   all attachments to application received
[]   details entered on case file list
[]   details entered on statistics list
[]   details entered on "Country information file"
[]   file opened
[]   copy of papers made for file
[]   if received from private individual, copy sent to Central Authority of requesting country

Location of child
[]   address of child is known
[]   Department of Immigration search requested

Convention requirements
[]   child under 16
[]   child habitually resident overseas
[]   applicant had rights of custody
[]   copy of relevant order/agreement enclosed
[]   applicant was exercising rights of custody

[]   application made within 12 months of removal
[]   application not made within 12 months of removal but explanation provided

[]   circumstances of removal show applicant did not acquiesce in removal
[]   circumstances of removal show applicant did acquiesce in removal but later withdrew
        consent
[]   circumstances of removal show applicant did acquiesce in removal but only for a limited
        period

[]   possible age/maturity of child (over 10) a factor
[]   possible harm/intolerable situation issues

[]   arrangements by applicant to pay return airfares

Processing
[]   consideration given to negotiating a voluntary return before starting proceedings
[]   application checked by legal officer
[]   application sent to regional central authority where child is located
[]   acknowledgment of receipt sent to requesting central authority or individual

On order for return (where abductor will return with children)
[]   relevant overseas Central Authority advised of impending return and asked to make
        contact with abductor
[]   details entered on statistics list

Appendix 3.5
Checklist of Convention Requirements
for Outgoing Application
(Paragraph 3.3)

HAGUE ABDUCTION APPLICATION - OUTGOING
(please keep this sheet on the inside cover of the file)

CHECKLIST OF REQUIREMENTS FOR OUTGOING HAGUE ABDUCTION APPLICATION -

Administrative
[]   all attachments to application received
[]   details entered on case file list
[]   details entered on statistics list
[]   details entered on "Country information file"
[]   file opened
[]   copy of papers made for file

Location of child
[]   address of child overseas certain _____ (country)
[]   Department of Immigration search requested

Convention requirements
[]   child under 16
[]   child habitually resident in _____ (country)
[]   applicant had rights of custody
[]   copy of relevant order/agreement enclosed
[]   applicant was exercising rights of custody

[]   application made within 12 months of removal
[]   application not made within 12 months of removal but explanation provided

[]   circumstances of removal show applicant did not acquiesce in removal
[]   circumstances of removal show applicant did acquiesce in removal but later withdrew consent
[]   circumstances of removal show applicant did acquiesce in removal but only for a limited period

[]   possible age/maturity of child (over 10) a factor
[]   possible harm/intolerable situation issues

[]   abductor has return ticket
[]   applicant can pay return airfares
[]   applicant advised to contact Office of Financial Assistance

Processing
[]   follow procedures in "Commonwealth Central Authority Guidelines" for applications to countries with specific requirements.
[]   covering letter to requested CA setting out custody rights
[]   consideration given to including 'advice to returning parent' with application
[]   application and covering letter checked by legal officer
[]   application sent to requested central authority
[]   acknowledgment sent to regional central authority/sender of the application

Appendix 3.6
Checklist of Convention Requirements
for Outgoing Application to Specific Country
(Paragraph 3.6)

HAGUE ABDUCTION APPLICATION - OUTGOING TO THE USA
(please keep this sheet on the inside cover of the file)

Administrative

[]   all attachments to application received
[]   file opened
[]   copy of papers made for file
[]   details entered on case file list
[]   details entered on statistics list

Location of child

[]   address of child in US certain
[]   Department of Immigration search requested

Convention requirements

[]   child under 16
[]   child habitually resident in _____ (country)
[]   applicant had rights of custody
[]   copy of relevant order/agreement enclosed
[]   applicant was exercising rights of custody
[]   application made within 12 months of removal
[]   application not made within 12 months of removal but explanation provided
[]   circumstances of removal show applicant did not acquiescence in removal
[]   circumstances of removal show applicant did acquiescence in removal but later withdrew consent
[]   circumstances of removal show applicant did acquiescence in removal but only for a limited period
[]   possible age/maturity of child (over 10) a factor
[]   possible harm/intolerable situation issues
[]   abductor has return ticket
[]   applicant can pay return airfares
[]   applicant advised to contact Office of Financial Assistance
[]   application for financial assistance included with application

Processing

[]   Follow special procedures in "Commonwealth Central Authority Guidelines" in relation to applications going to the US —
      []   does applicant have a US attorney?
      []   does applicant have capacity to pay an attorney in the US?
      []   does applicant think voluntary return could be negotiated?
      []   how was applicant made aware of respondent's address in US?
      []   coloured photograph of the child/ren included
[]   ask NCMEC to provide an estimate from any lawyer they nominate as to the likely cost and time of the proceedings
[]   covering letter to NCMEC setting out custody rights

[] consideration given to including 'advice to returning parent' with application
[] application and covering letter checked by legal officer
[] application sent to NCMEC
[] acknowledgment of receipt sent to regional central authority/sender of the application

Appendix 3.7
Checklist of Convention Requirements
for Outgoing Access Application
(Paragraphs 5.5 and 5.21)

HAGUE ACCESS APPLICATION - OUTGOING
(please keep this sheet on the inside cover of the file)

Application Received from: _____ (country)

Administrative

[]   all attachments to application received

[]   details entered on case file list

[]   details entered on statistics list

[]   details entered on "Country information file"

[]   file opened

[]   copy of papers made for file

Location of child

[]   address of child overseas certain _____ (country)

[]   Department of Immigration search requested

Convention requirements

[]   child under 16

[]   applicant has been refused access by custodial parent

[]   applicant has rights of access

[]   copy of relevant order/agreement enclosed

[]   applicant has no rights of access but seeks assistance to secure rights

[]   possible age/maturity of child (over 10) a factor

[]   undertaking by applicant to pay return airfares

Double checking

[]   application checked by legal officer

Processing

[]   application and covering letter checked by legal officer

[]   application sent to requested central authority

[]   acknowledgment sent to regional Central Authority or applicant

[]   if received from private individual, copy sent to relevant regional CA

Appendix 3.8
Checklist of Convention Requirements
for Incoming Access Application
(Paragraph 5.21)

HAGUE ACCESS APPLICATION - INCOMING
(please keep this sheet on the inside cover of the file)

Application received from: _____ (country)

Administrative

[]   administrative
[]   all attachments to application received
[]   details entered on case file list
[]   details entered on statistics list
[]   details entered on "Country information file"
[]   file opened
[]   copy of papers made for file
[]   if received from private individual, copy sent to Central Authority of requesting country

Location of child

[]   address of child in Australia is certain: _____
[]   Department of Immigration search requested

Convention requirements

[]   child under 16
[]   applicant has been refused access by custodial parent
[]   applicant has rights of access (in NZ cases)
[]   copy of relevant order/agreement enclosed
[]   applicant has no rights of access but seeks assistance to secure rights
[]   possible age/maturity of child (over 10) a factor
[]   undertaking by applicant to pay return airfares (if access is to be overseas)

Double checking

[]   application checked by legal officer

Processing

[]   consideration given to negotiating a voluntary agreement before starting proceedings
[]   application sent to regional central authority
[]   acknowledgment sent to relevant overseas central authority

On agreement/order for access

[]   requesting Central Authority advised of court decision or agreement
[]   details entered on statistics list

APPENDIX 4

SAMPLE LETTERS

Appendix 4.1
Acknowledgement Letter Requesting
Additional Information or Documents
(Paragraph 4.6)

Manitoba

JUSTICE   FAMILY LAW

705 – 405 Broadway
Winnipeg MB R3C 3L6
CANADA

Direct Line: (204) 945-
Facsimile: (204) 948-2004

File No.
In response, please reply to:

ATTENTION:

Dear Sir/Madam:

RE: Request for Return of   pursuant to the Hague *Convention on the Civil Aspects of International Child Abduction* ("the Hague *Convention*")

The Minister of Justice in the Province of Manitoba is charged with the responsibilities of the Central Authority for purposes of the above-referenced Hague *Convention*, within our province. Our office acts on the Minister's behalf in these matters and our Director, is shown as the contact person for purposes of the Central Authority for the Province of Manitoba in documentation at the Permanent Bureau at The Hague.

Further to the above-referenced Request for Return, I am forwarding a package of information relating to the Hague *Convention* which I hope will assist you in organizing the materials required to request the return of a child removed from your jurisdiction and believed to be in Manitoba. Enclosed you will find:

1.   A Schedule of Possible Undertakings, or conditions to which the party in your country may agree to be bound, so long as the other party returns the child to your jurisdiction forthwith;

2.   An example of an Affidavit in the form required by our Court.

We require an Affidavit sworn by the party in your country detailing the circumstances of the removal of the child, the nature of the parties' relationship, the status of any pending court proceedings in your jurisdiction, the existence of any court orders and whether any custody/access order is interim or final in nature. The Affidavit must specify the nature of the custody right that was being exercised immediately prior to the child's removal. The Affidavit must be sworn before a Notary Public and Court certified or notarial copies of any custody orders, and, if applicable, adoption orders, should be attached as exhibits to it. I will file these documents in the appropriate court in Manitoba in order to arrange a hearing on the Request for Return.

When preparing your client's Affidavit, it is important to stick to the facts and refrain from the use of conjecture, inflammatory language or opinion. If at all possible, send a draft of the Affidavit to my office via facsimile for review. I would be happy to assist you in addressing factual issues that can arise in the application of the Convention.

I appreciate that you may not have direct contact with the party in your country, and much of the information requested above is more readily obtained by the party's own solicitor. If the party's solicitor has already been made know to us, we will forward them a copy of this letter and enclosures, and trust that you will be in contact with that solicitor, for the purposes of coordinating your efforts in gathering the information we require.

We also require an Affidavit of law from a qualified person in your office or a legal expert in the area of child custody, describing your country's custody laws and confirming that, as those laws apply to the child in question, the child's removal from your country was wrongful within the meaning of the Hague *Convention*. Copies of relevant legislative provisions should be attached as exhibits to the Affidavit. This Affidavit must include the date on which the Request for Return was first received in your office and a photocopy of same should be attached as an exhibit. The Affidavit of law should also set forth the legal qualifications of the person swearing it, that person's association with your office, if applicable, and must also be sworn before a notary Public and conform with the enclosed sample. Note that a recent decision of the Manitoba Court of Queen's Bench affirmed by the Manitoba Court of Appeal suggests that it is preferable for the legal opinion to come from an independent lawyer – *i.e.* a lawyer other than counsel for the left behind parent.

With reference to any custody proceedings pending in your jurisdiction, I would ask that you please contact our office prior to pursuing an order of custody for your client, if one is not already in place. While it is not problematic to file an application for custody so as to be prepared for immediate action should the child be returned, a decision of the Supreme Court of Canada (*Thomson* v. *Thomson*, (1994) 6 R.F.L. (4th) 290) suggests that obtaining an order of custody in the originating jurisdiction before the child is returned may create unnecessary obstacles for your client.

Courts applying the Hague *Convention* increasingly look to undertakings made by the party seeking return, in order to minimize the possible impact on children. To that end, you or the party's counsel should canvass with the party in your country whether or not he/she is prepared to undertake to any of the terms outlined in the Schedule of Possible Undertakings that apply to this case. As each case is unique, many of the undertakings may no apply or other not listed may be more appropriate. Please provide me with the party's position regarding undertakings, in a letter separate from the Affidavit, as soon as possible.

Acting quickly can be critical in matters of this nature. However, it is still important that as much information as possible be provided. I hope this package is of assistance, and if you require any clarification, please do not hesitate to contact me. I look forward to receiving the party's documents shortly.

Yours truly,

Enclosure

cc: Solicitor of Party seeking return

Appendix 4.2
Letter Requesting Voluntary Return
(Paragraph 4.12)

UNITED STATES CENTRAL AUTHORITY
HAGUE CONVENTION ON THE CIVIL ASPECTS OF
INTERNATIONAL CHILD ABDUCTION
Office of Children's Issues, Room 2100
Bureau of Consular Affairs
Department of State
Washington, D.C. 20520
TEL: (202) 736-7000
FAX: (202) 312-9743

Dear   :

We are writing to inform you that the Government of   has forwarded to us an application from   who is seeking assistance under the Hague Convention on the Civil Aspects of International Child Abduction in returning   to   . We are requesting that in light of the Convention, you consider voluntarily agreeing to return the   to   in order to avoid the initiation of legal proceedings by the applicant under the Hague Convention in the United States.

On   , the 1980 Hague Convention on the Civil Aspects of International Child Abduction (copy enclosed) entered into force between the United States and   . Under Article 1 of the Convention, the United States is obliged to facilitate the prompt return of children removed to or retained in the United States. The Department of State, Office of Children's Issues, performs the functions of Central Authority for the United States. By agreement between the National Center for Missing and Exploited Children and the U.S. Central Authority, applications seeking the return of or access to children in the United States are processed by the National Center for Missing and Exploited Children. Pursuant to Article 10 of the Convention, the Central Authority of the State where the child is located must "take or cause to be taken all appropriate measures in order to obtain the voluntary return of the child."

Please note that the Convention does not specifically address the issue of who should have custody of the children, but rather deals with the question of where custody should be decided. The goal of the treaty is to protect children from the harmful effects of wrongful removal or retention by establishing procedures to ensure their prompt return to the country of their habitual residence, as well as to secure protection for rights of access. The Convention certainly envisions that the original taking parent may get custody once the children are returned. In fact, Article 19 of the Convention clearly states, "A decision under the Convention concerning the return of the child shall not be taken to be a determination on the merits of any custody issue."

If a voluntary return is not agreed to, legal proceedings under the Hague Convention may be initiated by   . We note that pursuant to the International Child Abduction Remedies Act (ICARA), 42 U.S.C. §11601-11610 (1988), which serves as the implementing law for this Convention, a court that orders return of the child under the Convention shall also order the taking party to pay necessary expenses incurred by or on behalf of the petitioner. Expenses may include: legal fees, court costs, foster home or other care during the course of the proceedings in the action, and transportation costs related to the return of the child, unless the taking party establishes that such an order would be clearly inappropriate.

In addition, the burden of proof for the petitioner in a Convention case is by a preponderance of the evidence, whereas the taking party claiming an exception set forth in Articles 13(b) or 20 of the Convention has the much more difficult burden of establishing their claim by clear and convincing evidence (§ 4(e) of ICARA).

For your convenience, we have enclosed a complete package of information concerning the Hague Convention. We encourage you to review this information carefully. After reviewing the information, we would appreciate it if you would advise   at the National Center for Missing & Exploited Children, 699 Prince Street, Alexandria, VA 22314 or (877) 446-2632, ext.   , by   as to when the   will be returned to   . Please indicate how   will be returned. If we have not received your response by   , or if you elect not to return the   to   , then we will be obliged under Article 7(f) of the Convention to facilitate the initiation of judicial proceedings by   to seek return of the   . Please do not hesitate to contact   if you have any further questions or need additional information.

We look forward to your favorable reply.

Sincerely,

Director
Office of Children's Issues
United States Central Authority

Enclosures: As stated

Appendix 4.3
Covering Letter For A Return Request
(Paragraph 3.5)

Australian Commonwealth Central Authority
Hague Convention on the Civil Aspects of International Child Abduction

Dear Sir

HAGUE CONVENTION ON THE CIVIL ASPECTS OF INTERNATIONAL CHILD ABDUCTION – A.Z & B.Z

1.   I attach a new application under the Hague Convention from Mrs X seeking the return to Australia of her children, AZ, born 23 October 1991, and BZ, born 14 July 1993, who have been wrongfully removed to France by their father, Mr Z.

2.   As you will see from the application, parenting orders have been made requiring the children to live with the mother and for the father to have contact. Under Australian law both parents retain parental responsibility for the children. Parental responsibility, which encompasses the Convention concept of rights of custody in Australia, is governed by a number of provisions of the Family Law Act 1975.

3.   Section 61B defines 'parental responsibility' in the following terms:

> 61B.   In this Part, 'parental responsibility', in relation to a child, means, all the duties, powers, responsibilities and authority which, by law, parents have in relation to children.

4.   Section 61C establishes the rights of parents:

> 61C(1) Each of the parents of a child who is not 18 has parental responsibility for the child.

> (2)   Subsection (1) has effect despite any changes in the nature of the relationships of the child's parents. It is not affected, for example, by the parents becoming separated or by either or both of them marrying or re-marrying.

(3)   Subsection (1) has effect subject to any order of a court for the time being in force (whether or not made under this Act and whether made before or after the commencement of this section).

5.   Section 111B(4)(a) provides additional confirmation that parents in Australia have 'rights of custody' within the meaning of the Hague Convention:

111B(4)   For the purposes of the Convention:

(a)   each of the parents of a child should be regarded as having rights of custody in respect of the child unless the parent has no parental responsibility for the child because of any order of a court for the time being in force; and

(b)   subject to any order of a court for the time being in force, a person who has a parenting order in relation to a child that is to any extent:

(i)   a residence order; or

(ii)   a specific issues order, under which the person is responsible for the day-to-day or long-term care, welfare and development of the child;

should be regarded as having rights of custody in respect of the child; and

(c)   subject to any order of a court for the time being in force, a person who has parental responsibility for a child because of the operation of this Act or another Australian law and is responsible for the day-to-day or long-term care, welfare and development of the child should be regarded as having rights of custody in respect of the child; and

(d)   subject to any order of a court for the time being in force, a person who has a contact order in relation to a child should be regarded as having a right of access to the child.

6.   The effect of sections 61C and 111B(4)(a) is that both parents of a child retain joint parental responsibility for the child until the child reaches the age of 18. In this case, the court has ordered that the children are to live with the mother, clearly showing that Mrs X continues to have joint parental responsibility for the children. Therefore, in this case, Mrs X has rights of custody in relation to the children. Mr Z's retention of the children in France is in breach of Mrs X's rights of custody within the meaning of Article 3 of the Convention.

7.   Attached is a copy of court orders made by the Family Court of Australia in relation to this matter on 14 January 2002.

8.   Attached is a document outlining services available to parents returning to New South Wales with children under the Convention. Please ensure this document is given to Mr Z with the application.

9.   I would be grateful if you would acknowledge receipt of the application. The contact officer in this matter is [...]. All correspondence on this matter should be addressed to him/her. His/her contact details are:

[...]

Thank you for your assistance.

Yours sincerely

Appendix 4.4
Letter Advising Applicant/Applicant's Lawyer of
Information Needed For An Application
(Paragraph 3.6)

Manitoba

JUSTICE   **FAMILY LAW**

705 – 405 Broadway
Winnipeg MB R3C 3L6
CANADA

Direct Line: (204) 945-
Facsimile: (204) 948-2004

File No.
In response, please reply to:

ATTENTION:

Dear Sir/Madam:

RE: The Hague Convention on the Civil Aspects of International Child Abduction ("The Hague Convention")

The Minister of Justice in the Province of Manitoba is charged with the responsibilities of the Central Authority for purposes of the above-referenced Hague *Convention*, within our province. Our office acts on the Minister's behalf in these matters and our Director is shown as the contact person for purposes of the Central Authority for the Province of Manitoba in documentation at the Permanent Bureau at The Hague.

Further to your recent inquiry, I am forwarding a package of information relating to The Hague *Convention*, which I hope will assist you in organizing the materials required to request the return of a child removed from Manitoba. Enclosed you will find:

1.   A pamphlet outlining some general information on The Hague *Convention*;

2.   An excerpt from *Family Law in Manitoba 2002*, on enforcement of custody and access rights generally in our province;

3.   A copy of Article 8 of The Hague *Convention*, which indicates the information that should be provided to Central Authorities when return is sought. The Hague *Convention* in its entirety is a schedule to *The Child Custody Enforcement Act* of Manitoba, C.C.S.M. c. C360;

4.   A blank Request for Return form;

5.   A Schedule of Possible Undertakings, or conditions to which your client may agree to be bound, so long as the other party returns the child to your jurisdiction forthwith.

You should complete the Request for Return form as soon as possible, and return same to my office for review. In addition, we require an Affidavit sworn by your client before a Notary Public, detailing the circumstances of the removal of the child, the nature of the parties' relationship, the status of any pending court proceedings in your jurisdiction, the existence of any court orders and whether any custody/access order is interim or final in nature. You must specify the nature of the custody right that was being exercised immediately prior to the child's removal. Court certified or notarial copies of any custody orders, and, if applicable, adoption orders, should be attached as exhibits to your client's Affidavit. Subject to the need for clarification or additional materials, I will transmit these documents to the Central Authority in the appropriate jurisdiction.

When preparing your client's Affidavit, it is important to stick to the facts and refrain from the use of conjecture, inflammatory language or opinion. If at all possible, send a draft of the Affidavit to my office via facsimile for review. I would be happy to assist you in addressing factual issues that can arise in the application of The Hague *Convention*.

With reference to any custody proceedings pending in Manitoba, I would ask that you please contact our office prior to pursuing an order of custody for your client, if one is not already in place. While it is not problematic to file an application for custody so as to be prepared for immediate action should the child be returned, a decision of the Supreme Court of Canada (*Thomson* v. *Thomson*, (1994) 6. R.F.L. (4th) 290) suggests that obtaining an order of custody in the originating jurisdiction before the child is returned may create unnecessary obstacles for your client.

Courts applying The Hague *Convention* increasingly look to undertakings made by the party seeking return, in order to minimize the possible impact on children. To that end, you should canvass with your client whether or not he/she is prepared to undertake to any of the terms outlined on the Schedule of Possible Undertakings that apply to your case. As each case is unique, many of the undertakings may not apply or others not listed may be more appropriate. Please provide me with your client's position regarding undertakings, in a letter separate from the Affidavit, as soon as possible.

I would urge you to review The Hague *Convention* in its entirety, and would point out that it does not treat breaches of rights of custody and rights of access in the same manner. To be familiar with other remedies that may be available and recent decisions in this area, you may also with to review the *Thomson* decision and the case comment on it by Professor James McLeod.

Finally, please be aware that many foreign jurisdictions do not have a system of legal aid such as exists in Manitoba. If children are located in a country to which the Hague *Convention* applies, your client may have to retain an attorney in the jurisdiction hearing the application. Given consideration to that issue now, if only in a preliminary way, may expedite matters for your client.

Acting quickly can be critical in matters of this nature. However, it is still important that your client provide as much information as possible. I hope this package is of assistance and if you require any clarification, please do not hesitate to contact me. I look forward to receiving your client's documents shortly.

Yours truly,

Enclosure

Appendix 4.5
Letter Requesting Voluntary Agreement
to Access Arrangements
(Paragraph 5.26)

NEW SOUTH WALES DEPARTMENT OF COMMUNITY SERVICES
STATE CENTRAL AUTHORITY FOR THE
HAGUE CONVENTION ON THE CIVIL ASPECTS OF
INTERNATIONAL CHILD ABDUCTION

[Date]

[Name]

[Address]

Dear

Re :   Hague Convention Application for access to KN

The Director-General of this Department is the State Central Authority for all matters arising under the Hague Convention on the Civil Aspects of Child Abduction in the State of NSW.

We have received an application under the Hague Convention from Mr. KN of New Zealand, to secure access to his daughter K who I understand is currently living with you.

Mr. K has made it clear that he is <u>not</u> seeking the return of K to New Zealand, but that he is simply wanting to have contact with K in accordance with the orders of the Otahuhu District Court made on 16 April 1999.

My purpose in writing to you is to ask whether you will agree to have consent orders made in the Family Court of Australia in the same terms of the orders of the Otahuhu Court. Unless I hear from you by <u>5.00 pm on 13th November 2001</u>, I will be filing a Hague Convention Application with the Family Court in Sydney and ask that the Court make the necessary access orders. I previously wrote to you on 27 September 2001, but have since been advised that the address I was given was incorrect.

The Hague Convention is a specialist area of law, and it is important that you get some legal advice in relation to this matter as soon as possible. You may wish to contact the NSW Legal Aid Commission and speak to a solicitor there. You may, of course, seek advice from any solicitor of your choice.

I look forward to hearing from you or your solicitor as soon as possible in the hope of resolving this matter as soon as possible.

Yours faithfully,

APPENDIX 5

MEASURES TAKEN BY CENTRAL AUTHORITIES

Appendix 5.1
Measures Taken By Central
Authorities to Help Locate Children
(Paragraph 4.10)

LIST OF MEASURES TAKEN BY CENTRAL AUTHORITIES
TO HELP LOCATE CHILDREN

1. Checking the Population Register (used by some European countries). People moving to a region are supposed to register, but it appears that there are no consequences for not doing so, and therefore this is not a reliable measure.

2. Enlist the aid of local police (if an address is known). The Italian Central Authority works well with local police.

3. Enlist the aid of the national police, as they often have a specialist unit for missing children matters or family matters.

4. In England and Wales and Australia, it is possible to apply to court to subpoena a person believed to have information about the location of a child. The person must then appear before the court and disclose the information.

5. In Quebec (Canada), there is a provincial police co-ordinator who will contact the local police to appoint a person to look for a child in a particular area.

6. Police in some countries can make discreet inquiries regarding a child.

7. National Center for Missing and Exploited Children (NCMEC) in the USA is a very effective locating agency with a wide variety of locating tools at its disposal.

NCMEC does not release any location information to the applicant, and only informs the lawyers for the purpose of serving court documents.

In some countries, it is possible to pay private investigators to assist in locating missing children. Some Central Authorities will pay the investigator's costs.

Appendix 5.2
Measures Taken by Central
Authorities to Assist a Safe Return
(Paragraph 3.18)

LIST OF VARIOUS PRACTICES UTILISED BY SOME CENTRAL AUTHORITIES (REQUESTED OR REQUESTING)

Notification of child protection bodies

- The obligation to ensure notification varies in different countries.
- Some States require notification in all cases concerning child protection. In other States, notification is required only when concerns are raised by the court or the Central Authority in the requested or requesting State.
- In other States, the Central Authority assumes no obligation to ensure notification occurs.

Provision of information in the requesting State

- Information on legal, financial, protection and other resources is made available to the returning parent.
- Some Central Authorities provide information to the left-behind parent.
- Others make available an information package to the taking parent as part of the application for return.

Facilitate contact with bodies providing such resources

- Contact is facilitated where possible.
- Intervention is often limited to referring the parents to information and services available.

Care for the child pending custody proceedings

- The requested Central Authority arranges to whom the child is entrusted for return.
- The requesting Central Authority co-ordinates arrangements for where and with whom the child stays after return until custody is decided.
- There is co-ordination between the Central Authorities and child protection authorities of the requested and requesting State to ensure the safety of the child.

Assistance for returning parent

- Support, advice or information is provided to a parent who accompanies the child on return
- Access to social services and counselling is provided or facilitated.
- Funding of the return is sought.

Assistance in ensuring respect for undertakings

- Mirror orders or safe harbour orders are encouraged.
- Competent court and relevant bodies are informed.
- Practical assistance and information is made available to the parent.
- Undertakings are made enforceable in limited circumstances.

APPENDIX 6

STATISTICS

FORM A1   Page ... of ...

ANNUAL STATISTICS RELATING TO THE HAGUE CONVENTION OF 25 OCTOBER 1980 ON THE CIVIL ASPECTS OF INTERNATIONAL CHILD ABDUCTION

REQUESTING CENTRAL AUTHORITY

CHILDREN TAKEN AWAY FROM .... (please fill in your country)

RETURN APPLICATIONS FOR THE YEAR ....

OTHER COUNTRY CONCERNED	NO. OF ACTIVE CASES		CASES REJECTED BY REQUESTED CENTRAL AUTHORITY	CHILD NOT TRACED	CHILD TRACED TO		CASES WITH-DRAWN	VOLU-NTARY RETURN	FINAL JUDICIAL ORDER		AVERAGE TIME BETWEEN RECEIPT OF APPLICATION AND FINAL JUDICIAL DETERMINATION	KNOWN CASES IN WHICH ORDER FOR RETURN NOT ENFORCED	CASES PENDING AT END OF YEAR
	CARRIED OVER FROM PREVIOUS YEAR	ARISING DURING YEAR			NON-CONVENTION COUNTRY	OTHER CONVENTION COUNTRY			RETURN	REFUSAL			
TOTAL													

FORM A2   Page ... of ...

ANNUAL STATISTICS RELATING TO THE HAGUE CONVENTION OF 25 OCTOBER 1980 ON THE CIVIL ASPECTS OF INTERNATIONAL CHILD ABDUCTION

REQUESTING CENTRAL AUTHORITY

CHILDREN BROUGHT TO .... (please fill in your country)

RETURN APPLICATIONS FOR THE YEAR ....

OTHER COUNTRY CONCERNED	NO. OF ACTIVE CASES		CASES REJECTED BY REQUESTED CENTRAL AUTHORITY	CHILD NOT TRACED	CHILD TRACED TO		CASES WITH-DRAWN	VOLU-NTARY RETURN	FINAL JUDICIAL ORDER		AVERAGE TIME BETWEEN RECEIPT OF APPLICATION AND FINAL JUDICIAL DETERMINATION	KNOWN CASES IN WHICH ORDER FOR RETURN NOT ENFORCED	CASES PENDING AT END OF YEAR
	CARRIED OVER FROM PREVIOUS YEAR	ARISING DURING YEAR			NON-CONVENTION COUNTRY	OTHER CONVENTION COUNTRY			RETURN	REFUSAL			
TOTAL													

APPENDIX 7

PUBLICATIONS AND INTERNET SITES DEALING WITH PREVENTION ISSUES

PUBLICATIONS AND INTERNET SITES DEALING WITH PREVENTION ISSUES

BRAND, I. - De preventie en repressie van internationale kinderontvoering in de Nederlandse wetgeving en rechtspraktijk; Leiden 1995 (doctoraalscriptie)

CANADA. Department of Foreign Affairs and International Trade: International Child Abductions: an manual for parents
>   Available from the website at:
>   http://www.voyage.gc.ca/Consular-   e/Publications/child_abductions-e.htm

CANADA. Our Missing Children/Nos Enfants Disparus Canada
>   http://www.ourmissingchildren.ca/en/publications/parent.html (English)
>   http://www.ourmissingchildren.ca/fr/publications/parental.html (French)

CHATIN, L. - Comment prévenir les déplacements ou les rétentions illicites d'enfants à l'étranger; Gazette du Palais, 1982, Nos 171 à 173, p. 2.

GERMANY. Der Generalbundesanwalt beim Bundesgerichtshof. Internationale Kindesentführung: Hinweise zur Rückführung aus dem Ausland und zur Durchsetzung des Umgangsrechts im Ausland. 1999.
>   Available from the website at:
>   http://www.bundeszentralregister.de/hkue_esue/broschuere.htm

JOHNSTON, J.R. & GIRDNER, L.K. - Early Identification of Parents at Risk for Custody Violations and Prevention of Child Abductions; Fam. & Conciliation Courts Review, 1998, p. 392.

MARX, A. - Internationale Kindesentführung - Ursachen, Prävention, Rückführung; *Braunschweiger Materialien zur Internationalen Sozialarbeit*, Heft 1, April 1998.

MOSTEN, F.S. - Mediation Makes Sense: How to Prevent an International Crisis; Family Advocate, 1993, p. 44.

NEAULT, J.-M. - L'enlèvement international d'un enfant par un parent: éléments de solution et de prévention; Développements récents en droit familial (1992), p. 231-332.

REUNITE: *Child Abduction Prevention Packs* (for England and Wales, Northern Ireland, Scotland, Spain) - available from the
>   Reunite website at http://www.reunite.org/prevention.html

U.S. STATE DEPARTMENT. Office of Childrens' Issues: International parental child abduction
>   Available from the website at http://www.travel.state.gov/int'lchildabduction.html

>   Part I: Prevention - How to Guard Against International Child Abduction (specific web link: http://www.travel.state.gov/int'lchildabduction.html#part1)

COUNTRY LINKS and PREVENTION LINKS:

Argentina	http://www.menores.gov.ar/ http://www.menores.gov.ar/ingles/index1.htm
Australia	http://www.law.gov.au/childabduction/index.html

link to section on emergency contacts	http://www.law.gov.au/childabduction/contactemerg.html
Austria	http://www.justiz.gv.at/
Belgium	http://www.just.fgov.be
Canada	http://www.dfait-maeci.gc.ca
link to section on preventive measures (Consular Affairs website)	http://www.voyage.gc.ca/Consular-e/Publications/child_abductions-e.htm#1 http://www.voyage.gc.ca/Consular-e/Publications/child_abductions-e.htm#7
Canada - Quebec	http://www.justice.gouv.qc.ca/special/anglais/eie-a/preventive-a.htm http://www.justice.gouv.qc.ca/francais/ministere/dossiers/eie/mesures.htm
Canada - Missing Children Network	http://www.missingchildren.ca/MCN.htm?CD=13 (for link to 'Safeguards against abduction)
China – Hong Kong	http://www.info.gov.hk/justice/
link to section on preventive measures link to Immigration Department's assistance	http://www.info.gov.hk/justice/childabduct/english/abduct_riprevent.html http://www.info.gov.hk/justice/childabduct/english/abduct_riidassist.html
Denmark	http://www.civildir.dk/ publikationer (See *Internationale børnebortførelser,* and *International child abduction*)
Finland	http://www.om.fi/
links to section on preventive measures	http://www.om.fi/9604.htm#prevent (English) http://www.om.fi/9439.htm (Swedish) http://www.om.fi/3891.htm (Finnish) http://www.om.fi/uploads/s74gyb9bp2c9aup.pdf (Russian)
France	http://www.diplomatie.gouv.fr/francais/FAMILLES/enlevements/ actualites.htm
link to section on preventive measures	http://www.diplomatie.gouv.fr/francais/FAMILLES/enlevements/ prevenir_00.html
Germany	http://www.bundeszentralregister.de/ (Central Authority) http://www.auswaertiges-amt.de/www/en/laenderinfos/konsulat/kindesentziehung_html (Federal Foreign Office - in English)

link to section on preventive measures	http://www.bundeszentralregister.de/hkue_esue/broschuere.htm#Vorbeugung
New Zealand link to section on preventive measures	http://www.courts.govt.nz http://www.courts.govt.nz/family/hague_convention.html http://www.passports.govt.nz/diawebsite.nsf/wpg_URL/Services-Passports-Preventing-Children-Being-Taken-from-New-Zealand?OpenDocument
Spain	http://www.mju.es/cooperacion_juridica/g_sustmenores.htm
Switzerland	http://www.ofj.admin.ch
link to section on preventive measures	http://www.ofj.admin.ch/f/index.html (for link to aide memoire on prevention) http://www.ofj.admin.ch/themen/lkidnapping/intro-f.htm
UK – England and Wales	http://www.offsol.demon.co.uk/
link to section on preventive measures	http://www.fco.gov.uk (search on 'abduction' for advice on prevention)
USA – State Department	http://www.travel.state.gov
link to section on preventive measures	http://www.travel.state.gov/int'lchildabduction.html#part1
USA – NCMEC	http://icmec.missingkids.com/

OTHER SERVICES PROVIDED BY THE PERMANENT BUREAU OF THE HAGUE CONFERENCE ON PRIVATE INTERNATIONAL LAW

The Hague Conference on Private International Law: <http://www.hcch.net>

The Child Abduction Home Page: <http://www.hcch.net/e/conventions/menu28e.html>
The text of the *Hague Convention of 25 October 1980 on the Civil Aspects of International Child Abduction*: <http://www.hcch.net/e/conventions/text28e.html>

Explanatory Report of the Convention [Pérez-Vera Report]:
<http://www.hcch.net/e/conventions/expl28e.html>

Special Commissions to Review the Operation of the *Hague Convention of 25 October on the Civil Aspects of International Child Abduction*:
<http://www.hcch.net/e/conventions/reports28e.html>

Electronic versions of the Guide to Good Practice:
<http://www.hcch.net/e/conventions/guide28e.html>

Responses to the standard questionnaire for newly acceding States:
<http://www.hcch.net/e/conventions/guide28e.html>

Central Authorities designated under the Convention:
<http://www.hcch.net/e/authorities/caabduct.html>

Full status of the Convention:
<http://www.hcch.net/e/status/stat28e.html>

Concise status of the Convention:
<http://www.hcch.net/e/status/abdshte.html>

The International Child Abduction Database (INCADAT):
<http://www.incadat.com>

The Hague Project for International Co-operation and the Protection of Children:
<http://www.hcch.net/e/conventions/project.html>

Conclusions and Recommendations from Judicial Seminars on the International Protection of Children:
<http://www.hcch.net/e/conventions/seminar.html>

The Judges' Newsletter on International Child Protection:
<http://www.hcch.net/e/conventions/news28e.html>

Bibliography:

<http://www.hcch.net/e/conventions/bibl28e.html>

Links to related websites:

<http://www.hcch.net/e/conventions/links28e.html>

Contact details for the Permanent Bureau of the Hague Conference are as follows:

Hague Conference on Private International Law

Permanent Bureau

Scheveningseweg 6

2517 KT The Hague

The Netherlands

Tel.: +31 (70) 363 3303

Fax: +31 (70) 360 4867

Email: secretariat@hcch.net